EDGAR PAYNE

The Scenic Journey

Pomegranate

PORTLAND, OREGON

EDGAR PAYNE

The Scenic Journey

Scott A. Shields, PhD
and
Patricia Trenton, PhD

with additional essays by

Lisa N. Peters, PhD

Peter H. Hassrick

Jean Stern

Preface by Jenkins Shannon

Pasadena Museum of California Art | Pomegranate Communications, Inc.

Published by Pomegranate Communications, Inc.
19018 NE Portal Way, Portland, OR 97230
800-227-1428   pomegranate.com

Published on the occasion of the exhibition *Edgar Payne: The Scenic Journey*

Crocker Art Museum, Sacramento, California
February 11, 2012–May 6, 2012

Pasadena Museum of California Art, Pasadena, California
June 3, 2012–October 14, 2012

Gilcrease Museum, Tulsa, Oklahoma
December 1, 2012–March 24, 2013

Unless otherwise indicated, works of art are by Edgar Payne.
Measurements are in inches; height precedes width.

Jacket image: *Sunset, Canyon de Chelly,* 1916. Oil on canvas, 28 x 34 in. Mark C. Pigott Collection
Frontispiece: *The Rendezvous (Santa Cruz Island, CA)* (detail, pp. 54–55), 1915. Oil on canvas, 33 x 42 in. Private collection

Library of Congress Cataloging-in-Publication Data
Shields, Scott A.
  Edgar Payne : the scenic journey / Scott A. Shields and Patricia Trenton ; with essays by Lisa Peters, Peter H. Hassrick, Jean Stern ; preface by Jenkins Shannon ; introduction by Patricia Trenton.
      p. cm.
  Published on the occasion of an exhibition held at the Crocker Art Museum, Sacramento, Calif., Feb. 11, 2012–May 6, 2012, the Pasadena Museum of California Art, Pasadena, Calif., June 3, 2012–Oct. 14, 2012, and the Gilcrease Museum, Tulsa, Okla., Dec. 1, 2012–Mar. 24, 2013.
  Includes bibliographical references and index.
  ISBN 978-0-7649-6053-6 (hardcover)
  1. Payne, Edgar A. (Edgar Alwin), 1882–1947—Exhibitions. 2. Landscapes in art—Exhibitions. I. Payne, Edgar A. (Edgar Alwin), 1882–1947. II. Trenton, Patricia. III. Peters, Lisa. IV. Hassrick, Peter H. V. Stern, Jean, 1946– VI. Pasadena Museum of California Art. VII. Thomas Gilcrease Institute of American History and Art. VIII. Crocker Art Museum. IX. Title.

N6537.P32A4 2012
759.13—dc23
                              2011025192

Item No. A203
Designed by Patrice Morris

Printed in China

31 30 29 28 27 26 25 24 23 22   16 15 14 13 12 11 10 9 8 7

CONTENTS

PREFACE AND ACKNOWLEDGMENTS

Edgar Payne: The Scenic Journey is the largest exhibition ever organized by the Pasadena Museum of California Art (PMCA) and thus fittingly marks the museum's tenth anniversary. Since opening in 2002, the PMCA has championed the work of California's artists, particularly those who have been inspired by the state's natural beauty. Although many California artists helped to establish this rich artistic tradition, the decision to feature Edgar Payne's glorious vistas on our tenth anniversary was an obvious one.

Characterized by an aesthetic of power and dynamism, Payne's work is distinct from the quieter and more picturesque depictions of modern life and landscape made famous by nineteenth-century French Impressionists. An avid traveler, the artist sought vitality in the landscapes he featured and was among the first painters to trek through the Sierra Nevada in search of rugged beauty. His travels through the Southwest resulted in equally sublime depictions of the desert, and in Europe he rendered the towering peaks of the Alps as well as the colorful harbors of France and Italy. This retrospective examines the beauty and breadth of Payne's work.

The decision to organize an Edgar Payne exhibition was met with overwhelming support from the PMCA's board of directors as well as from other art institutions, scholars, and collectors. This project would not have been possible without Scott A. Shields, PhD, associate director and chief curator of the Crocker Art Museum in Sacramento. One of the foremost scholars on California art and curator of the exhibition, Shields wrote the lead essay and the chronology for this catalogue. We are thrilled that the exhibition will premiere at the Crocker, the first public art museum in the West, in February 2012, before opening at the PMCA in June 2012.

The PMCA is also extremely grateful for the help of esteemed art historian Patricia Trenton, PhD, who served as the project's senior advisor. Trenton not only sought out the work and assembled the checklist for the exhibition but also wrote the introduction and provided invaluable guidance in producing this catalogue. The success of this project is largely due to her knowledge and insight.

We also thank Peter H. Hassrick; Lisa N. Peters, PhD; and Jean Stern for the essays that they contributed. Hassrick focused on Payne's work in the American Southwest, Peters on Payne's European production, and Stern on the relationship between Payne's paintings and his

Mt. Ritter and Lake Ediza, n.d. Oil on canvas, 48 x 48 in. Collection of Mr. and Mrs. Jon R. Stuart

photography. Together with Shields and Trenton, these three accomplished scholars bring new information and deeper understanding to the work of this versatile artist.

We gratefully acknowledge the assistance of Dewitt Clinton McCall III of DeRu's Fine Arts, the keeper of archival material received from Payne's daughter. We are indebted to McCall's generosity and his willingness to share information and early photographs. Access to these materials provided critically important information to our essayists. We would also like to acknowledge the late Rena Neumann Coen, who wrote the seminal 1988 book *The Paynes, Edgar & Elsie: American Artists,* from which our essayists drew valuable information.

The scope and scale of this exhibition and catalogue would not have been realized without the support of two additional venues—the Crocker Art Museum in Sacramento, California, and the Gilcrease Museum in Tulsa, Oklahoma. I would like to thank their respective directors, Lial A. Jones and Duane H. King, PhD, for their willingness to collaborate on this project. I am particularly grateful to Jon R. Stuart, trustee of the Gilcrease Museum, for his assistance in making this venue possible.

In addition, I would like to thank Pomegranate Communications, Inc., in Petaluma, California, led by publisher Katie Burke. Gerard Vuilleumier deserves special thanks for traveling far and wide to photograph the paintings. We also thank Christopher Bliss and Sue Ganz for photographing a number of the paintings and Lilli Colton for her preliminary management of the catalogue. Particular thanks go to Eric Jessen, museum environmental consultant and retired chief of the Orange County Harbors, Beaches and Parks Department, for his explorations of the Sierra Nevada and the Laguna coast in order to confirm the veracity and subject matter of numerous paintings. We also thank Jim Staub of the California Institute of Technology for researching the types of cameras that Payne might have used.

We are grateful to many individuals and institutions who have lent from their collections and provided images for the exhibition; some lent multiple pieces and agreed to part with them for a significant period of time. We also thank the individuals who helped locate these collections as well as key works of art. Their support has contributed to the quality and success of the exhibition.

Producing an exhibition and its catalogue requires significant resources, and fortunately the PMCA has many patrons who are dedicated to the arts and have come forward in celebration of Edgar Payne. Our special thanks and appreciation are directed to Mark Pigott for his visionary and generous support as the presenting sponsor. His significant contribution not only allowed us to realize the exhibition but also ensured the publication of this book, the first comprehensive review of Payne's remarkable career.

We are also extremely grateful to our underwriting supporters—the Historical Collections Council of California Art, Barbara and Michael Brickman, Simon K. Chiu, Jeff Dutra, Robert Giem, Christine and Reed Halladay, Cathie and David Partridge, Ray Redfern of Redfern Gallery, Donna and Mark Salzberg, Mr. and Mrs. Thomas B. Stiles II, and Anonymous. Without their contributions at the early planning stages, this exhibition would not have been possible.

The Jonathan Heritage Foundation, the MacTon Foundation, Kathleen and Paul Bagley, Yvonne J. Boseker, Bente and Gerald Buck, W. C. Foxley, Linda and Jim Freund, Whitney Ganz, Nadine and Robert J. Hall, Ruth and Robert Mirvis, Elma and Earl Payton, Earlene and Herb Seymour, Bernard Vandeuren, Gerard Vuilleumier, Bonhams & Butterfields, Christie's, George Stern Fine Arts, Heritage Auctions, John Moran Auctioneers, Josh Hardy Galleries, and Steven Stern, California Paintings also contributed greatly to this endeavor.

We are also grateful for the work of the PMCA's board of directors. Simon K. Chiu endorsed this exhibition from the outset and helped with the museum's fund-raising efforts; David Partridge, chairman of the board, Reed Halladay, chairman emeritus, and Bob and Arlene Oltman, founders of the PMCA, also championed this exhibition and lent support. Other significant contributors include Crocker Art Museum staff Erin Aitali, Andrew Blicharz, and Diana Daniels, as well as PMCA staff members Shirlae Cheng-Lifshin, Emma Jacobson-Sive, Christine Goo, Diana Ajuria, and Alexis Kaneshiro. We thank them and many others who have lent their assistance.

Finally, we thank Edgar Payne for producing paintings that are not only beautiful but also diverse and far-reaching. It is our hope that the breadth and scope of this exhibition and catalogue will enhance understanding of this boldly peripatetic artist and do justice to his extraordinary work.

Jenkins Shannon
Executive Director
Pasadena Museum of California Art

Introduction

EDGAR PAYNE
THE ARTIST HIMSELF

Patricia Trenton, PhD
Senior Advisor, *Edgar Payne: The Scenic Journey*

Edgar Payne created scores of paintings depicting various scenes in America and Europe, notably Sierra Nevada and Alpine mountainscapes that caught his eye, Italian and French marinescapes with boats and fishermen, and Southwest desert scenes populated with distant Native American figures on horseback. Known as "an indefatigable worker in his chosen profession," he assimilated every bit of knowledge that he acquired from each picture, whether successful or experimental.[1]

Called the poet-painter of the California Sierra, Payne led a close circle of artistic friends on treks through the indomitable Sierra country, drawing on his pathfinding skills and knowledge of the area to introduce them to new subjects for their brushes.[2]

In both America and Europe, the remoteness of the mountains attracted him. Perhaps, as Scott A. Shields suggests in his essay, they represented an escape from the turmoil of urban settlements, a respite of solitude and meditation. Perhaps Payne was inspired by the challenge of conquering great heights as a means of proving his virility and technical skills or of capturing unique, sublime, and picturesque views of previously unknown vistas. His first recorded venture into the majestic Sierra country, in 1917, was somewhat early and unusual for an artist in Southern California, reflecting his adventurous, imaginative, and independent spirit. Though he never conquered the reaches of the summits, he viewed his scenes from the heights of valleys just below, setting up campsites with his entourage.

From the published writings of his wife, Elsie Palmer Payne, and his daughter, Evelyn Payne Hatcher, I learned that Edgar Payne rose above his meager beginnings to become an industrious, self-motivated achiever, completely absorbed in his devotion to artistic pursuits. Family apparently played a secondary role in his life; his work was always the primary focus. Elsie was a loving wife who sacrificed and sublimated her own art career for her husband's, while Edgar was constantly on the move in search of new sights and challenges. Even his daughter's schooling had to accommodate his frantic schedule and ever-changing itinerary.

Laguna Coastline (detail, pp. 64–65), n.d.

Profile View of Seated Navajo, n.d. Photograph by Edgar Payne. Courtesy of DeRu's Fine Arts

Payne's daughter gave the family's archival material to the owner of DeRu's Fine Arts, Dewitt Clinton McCall III, who handled her father's work during her later years. This archive reveals another dimension of Payne's talents: his technical and mechanical skills. In reviewing the large, artistically composed photographs Payne took in the High Sierra, the Southwest, and Europe, I learned that he employed a complex method using the bellows of his camera to develop and enlarge his photographs. Reflecting his curiosity and insistence on accuracy, these images served as the basis for several of his most outstanding paintings—including his complex compositions of Chioggia and Brittany showing numerous figures and boats intertwined at sea and home port.

His photographs of Navajos mounted on horseback, seated, or in portrait poses, taken in the Southwest in the 1920s and 1930s, are equally compelling (opposite). Yet he rarely used them as the basis for his Southwest paintings, which typically feature small figures on horseback dwarfed by the desolate, rugged desert landscape. Perhaps, as his daughter later remarked, this was meant to express Payne's belief that human life was "subordinate" to the landscape.[3]

In looking through the many color and black-and-white sketches and finished drawings of sites and subjects in the archive, I noted how carefully Payne studied and recorded detailed features and aspects of perspective in order to accurately transfer them to canvas. His many small pencil sketches and oil studies offer insight into how he created his finished works.

Further underlining Payne's multifaceted talents are an intricately carved model of a French yawl tuna boat, with accurate riggings and scale, and a four-sided, painted wood sculpture derisively called the *"Bird House"*—a most complicated piece indeed (p. 14). True to the Arts and Crafts aesthetic, Payne also designed and constructed hand-carved wood furniture with cast metal fittings in the Moorish and Renaissance styles (p. 15), as well as many varieties of carved gold-leaf frames for his pictures. These pieces demonstrate the consummate craftsmanship and almost scientific care he devoted to developing his artistic creations in other media.

Seeing this remarkably intact archive of creative and ephemeral materials, letters, and critical notices was a revelation, one that gave me a broader perspective and a deeper insight into the artist's work and persona. It also gave the essayists in this volume a more realistic perspective of the flowery and often misinterpreted accounts written by the art critics of the period. A large scrapbook compiled by the artist's wife, containing critical reviews, notices, letters, and awards, greatly facilitated their research efforts.

In 1941, Payne produced a book, *Composition of Outdoor Painting*—a training guide for students of art that is now in its seventh edition. Today, it is obvious why he published this treatise on the principles of drawing, painting, and the use of perspective: it was a defensive reaction to what he saw happening to art in America. A few years earlier, in 1939, he and a group of conservative artists had founded the Los Angeles branch of the Society for Sanity in Art, an organized reaction to the modern American ideas and techniques being adopted by many artists. Payne was even its president for a short period.

Composition of Outdoor Painting gave Payne a vehicle for combating what he viewed as a total disregard for the fundamentals of drawing and painting. He followed the book with a series of lectures

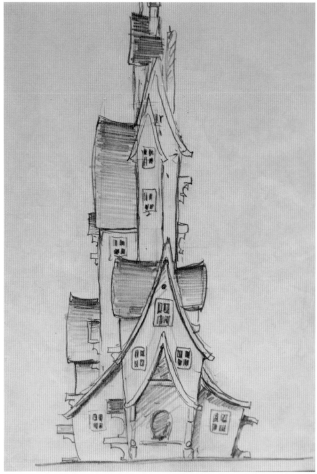

Above: *Idea Drawing for a Wood Sculpture*, c. 1925.
Pencil on paper, 11 x 9 in. Courtesy of DeRu's Fine Arts

Left: *Sculpture ("Bird House")*, c. 1925. Painted wood,
60 x 24 x 24 in. Collection of Thomas T. Tatum

Above: *Small Chest,* n.d.
Wood, 16 x 27 x 15 in.
Courtesy of DeRu's Fine Arts

Right: *Hexagonal Table,* n.d.
Wood, 32 x 30 x 30 in.
Courtesy of DeRu's Fine Arts

Arizona Clouds, n.d. Oil on canvas, 28 x 34 in. Collection of Paul and Kathleen Bagley

demonstrating these principles. To further elaborate on his treatise, Payne and his nephew Ralph Payne produced a short 16 mm color movie, narrated by Lyle Bond and with an original score by Alexander Borisoff, titled *Sierra Journey.* Debuting in March 1946, it was a "scenic picture of the rugged California mountains as seen through the artist's eyes" and starred Payne, of course, painting on site.[4]

With the rise of modernism, the works of Payne and other historic plein-air artists of Southern California fell out of vogue and into obscurity. Little more was published on these artists until 1988, when, assisted by Evelyn Payne Hatcher and drawing on archival material gathered by Evelyn's husband, Rena Neumann Coen wrote a seminal book, *The Paynes, Edgar & Elsie: American Artists.* In 2002, Evelyn revealed another dimension of the artist by publishing

a book on her father's drawings, featuring those that remained in the estate. Since the publication of these works, new information, found both in the archive and through global sources via the Internet, has come to light and enriched our understanding of Payne and his career. That story is told here.

In these pages, readers can travel along on the scenic journey of Edgar Payne's life and, it is hoped, gain a wider appreciation of his multifaceted talents. A painter, writer, craftsman, photographer, explorer, and leader, he embodied the definition of a Renaissance man. While many of his contemporaries were content to focus solely on their artistic production, this was not enough for Payne. He believed that his legacy lay not only in his painting but also in his life and the example it set for others. It is this approach that has secured his place in the broader annals of California art.

NOTES

1. Elizabeth Bingham, Art Exhibits and Comment, *Saturday Night,* February 11, 1922.

2. Fred Hogue, "Grandeur of California Sierras: Paints Sunset Glow and Morning Light," *Hemet (CA) News,* July 1, 1927, courtesy of Archives of American Art, microfilm #2721, Smithsonian Institution.

3. Evelyn Payne Hatcher, "Edgar Payne: Biographical Notes," unpublished typescript, Edgar and Elsie Palmer Payne Papers, DeRu's Fine Arts, Bellflower, CA.

4. Payne Pictorials, announcement of screening of *Sierra Journey* to be held at Bell and Howell Auditorium, Los Angeles, March 1, 1946, Edgar and Elsie Palmer Payne Papers, DeRu's Fine Arts, Bellflower, CA.

EDGAR PAYNE
THE SCENIC JOURNEY

Scott A. Shields, PhD

Associate Director and Chief Curator
Crocker Art Museum

As went "the rolling stone, the floating cloud, the vagrant bee," so Edgar Alwin Payne painted "as Homer sang, wandering from place to place where his fancy moved him."[1] In the course of his painting expeditions, his journeys covered some 100,000 miles throughout the United States and Europe.[2] He found magnificence in diverse settings, including the Southern and Central California coast, the Sierra Nevada, the Swiss Alps, the harbors and waterways of France and Italy, and the desert Southwest. In each locale, he sought vitality, bigness, nobility, and grandeur, which he turned into unified, carefully calculated compositions with brushwork that seemed to pulsate with life.[3]

Described as a "seeker" and an "adventurous wanderer," the artist was more reserved than his travels or paintings would imply.[4] He was modest and quiet, succinct and focused. Always striving to "mix brains with paint," he chose his words carefully, just as he assiduously selected the compositional elements for his paintings.[5] He had many friends and admirers who found his drive, determination, and talent compelling; they sought his advice, followed his lead in founding various arts organizations, and even traveled with him to the remotest wilderness. Those who knew him best, however, also noted that he appeared out of place in a crowd, in big cities especially, and seemed most at home in the highest reaches of the mountains or the enormity of the desert.[6] Nothing in his dress or sensible haircut suggested an artist, yet art was the most important thing in his life, and he worked hard and consistently at it (p. 22).[7] Everything else, including his family, came second. On the day of his wedding, he asked his bride, Elsie Palmer, if they could change the time of the event because the "light was right" for painting.[8] An artist herself, Palmer understood and consented (p. 23).

Born March 1, 1883, near Cassville, in Barry County, Missouri, Payne grew up in the Ozark Mountains.[9] His upbringing was certainly far removed from the mainstream of art; nevertheless, he entered the world during a period of great aesthetic upheaval, one that would eventually shape and color his own production. In 1878, the Society of American Artists officially separated from the National Academy of Design. The National Academy was conservative and encumbering, and the Society wanted an alternative, one that sanctioned more innovative approaches. The Society's summation "that art legitimately concerns itself only with the felicitous arrangement of color and line; that its only proper aim is technical excellence and its only fit audience connoisseurs" was a blatant rejection of the more established style practiced by artists of the Hudson River School.[10] A generational rift was forming, placing the "new men" and the "old men" at opposites.[11]

Among painting genres, landscape in particular experienced momentous change. The tight literalism and leaf-by-leaf detail that English critic John Ruskin endorsed was supplanted by freer paint handling,

P. 18: *The Topmost Sierra* (detail, p. 74), c. 1921

Opposite: *Capistrano Canyon* (detail, p. 41), n.d.

Edgar Payne, 1926. Photograph by George E. Hurrell (American, 1904–1992). Courtesy of DeRu's Fine Arts

Edgar and Elsie Payne, 1913. Photographer unknown. Courtesy of DeRu's Fine Arts

Untitled [Eucalyptus Landscape, California], n.d. Oil on canvas, 32 x 40 in. Private collection

more pronounced abstraction, and greater investiture of emotional content. Whereas earlier landscape painters had suppressed their own personalities in favor of precise representation, as the twentieth century dawned artists championed the more intimate, personal touch of the individual over painting that fulfilled a didactic, moral, or utilitarian function. It was a trend known as *l'art pour l'art,* or "art for art's sake," and it was famously endorsed by poet Théophile Gautier, painter James McNeill Whistler, and others. While Payne absolutely agreed that paintings should be translations of nature, not transcriptions, he also believed firmly in "truth and fact."[12]

In the move away from literalism, artists turned their backs on panoramic, boldly encompassing depictions of nature in favor of more intimate, human-scaled environs. At the nineteenth century's close, the landscapes of artists nationwide became more accessible, quiet, and introspective, supplanting the grandiose theatricality and sublimity of the Hudson River School. This was certainly true in Northern California until the 1910s, but at the same moment in Southern California many artists sought a grander scheme with new techniques and greater emphasis on light and color. There, according to writer George Wharton James, "colours simple and complex, harmonizing and clashing, separate and combined, loud and soft, timid and bold, exuberant and quiet; colours of dignity and colours of frivolity, of pride and humility,—but all . . . glorious" seemed to be everywhere one turned.[13] This color was exploited by a new generation of California artists, including Payne, who together have been labeled Impressionists.

When Impressionism finally reached California, it was a mainstream style throughout Europe and the East Coast. In the Golden State, Impressionism concluded a stylistic progression from the north to the south, which began with highly detailed images of California's majestic Sierra Nevada scenery, evolved into Barbizon School–inspired and Tonalist landscapes of the San Francisco region and the central coast, and culminated in Southern California plein-air scenes of mountains, desert, and sea. The 1915 Panama-Pacific International Exposition in San Francisco provided the defining moment for Impressionism in the state, especially for northern painters but also for artists from the Los Angeles region—including not only Payne but also Maurice Braun, Benjamin Brown, Granville Redmond, Guy Rose, Donna Schuster, William Wendt, and numerous others—who participated in, visited, and even helped jury the exposition. Confronted with the work of the international avant-garde, artists broadly took stock of their own production, and many broke with the past and forayed into color and abstraction. In 1916, critic Laura Bride Powers announced that California's "blue and gold and crimson, flashing color from field and sky and ocean, holds a lure for her artist children. And answering the world's cry for color—and more color—they paint what they see. They cannot resist it."[14] The following year, Antony Anderson, self-proclaimed "Art Critic of the West," expressed a similar view. "There was a time when artists thought they could paint without light, and when air was hardly considered. That time seems prehistoric to us now, but it was really only a few years ago. Today the search for light and air is pursued with enthusiasm, and we refuse to consider seriously the picture that is without them."[15]

Ideologically, the leap from the Hudson River School to Barbizon and Tonalism and then to Impressionism, at least for most Californians, was not that great. At the heart of each was a profound reverence for the landscape of California and a yearning to communicate its abundant glories. Subject matter remained essentially unchanged: the Sierra, rolling hills, expressive trees,

the coast, and views of the sea were all still popular. Only the treatment was different, with a greater emphasis than before on wildflowers painted in glorious profusion, a trend especially popular in Southern California. Although flowers were of little interest to Payne, he was one of the leading painters in the Southland to find new viability in grander-scale mountain subjects, even though the majority of the preceding generation's painters—most notably former Sierra specialist William Keith in San Francisco—had declared such subjects "unpaintable." It took an Indiana painter,

Arched Trees, n.d. Pencil on paper, 8 x 10 in. Collection of Mr. and Mrs. Jon R. Stuart

Theodore Steele, who came to California in 1892, to envision the possibilities:

> I do not think his [Keith's] conclusions that these subjects are unpaintable is correct, but they will be painted by artists of the Monet type, for one can see Monets everywhere. The same color charged air, the same scintillating radiance that Monet finds in the south of France, though with nobler forms and greater compositions than one usually finds in his pictures. I have no shadow of a doubt that some day there will develop a school of painters on this western coast, that can fully interpret these great subjects, and give to the world a new and powerful school of art.[16]

Payne kept pace with stylistic trends by abandoning literalism and taking joy in color and, especially, in the application of pigment, which he believed to be an important component of beautiful painting.[17] The animated daubs and swipes of his brush were contrary to the nearly invisible brushwork of previous California painters, and as Payne's career progressed, these grew bolder, even mosaic-like, an approach that critic Antony Anderson found to resemble "old Oriental rugs" (right).[18]

Payne's aesthetic, however, was perfectly in keeping with Southern California's scintillating light and color. The region was in fact ideal for landscape painting. A 1920 article in *California Southland* stated that California's "brilliant sunshine, the dry air, and the resultant sparkle and color have inspired the inhabitants to express their love of country in paint and dye."[19] Antony Anderson recognized that "nature has been magnificently and prodigally kind to us out here; we have everything in landscape that the eye could wish for, and we find transcendent beauty wherever we turn to look for it. Too, the climatic conditions are ideal for the landscape painter—sunshine perennial, 365 working days, or nearly so many."[20] Another writer, Everett C. Maxwell, found it inevitable that in this "land of golden light and purple shadows," a new school of landscape painting would flower.[21]

Responding to the light, Payne worked with pure, saturated hues. Fred Hogue, chief editorial writer for the *Los Angeles Times,* called Payne a "poet who sings in colors."[22] With the brilliant turquoise of the ocean, hills gold in summer and acid green in winter, and colorful rock formations in the Sierra, Payne was presented with opportunity at every turn. Like the French Impressionists, he avoided black, creating neutral shades by combining complementary colors even for the darkest shadows. For him, California's topography

Canyon Riders (detail, p. 184), n.d.

Hills of Altadena, 1917–1919. Oil on canvas, 36 x 45 in. Steven Stern Collection

Capistrano Canyon, n.d. Oil on canvas, 24 x 28 in. Private collection. Courtesy of The Irvine Museum

Sycamore in Autumn, Orange County Park, c. 1917. Oil on board, 32 x 42 in. Private collection. Courtesy of The Irvine Museum held more brilliance than did landscapes abroad. "The rocks of the Alps are granite, of a uniform gray," he explained. "In the Sierras one finds mineral ledges everywhere. There is a diversity of color. There are reds and greens not to be found anywhere in Europe. One finds here the mountains of Switzerland under the skies of Italy."[23]

Despite his progressive palette and technique, Payne pursued Impressionism by looking backward as much as forward. He thought of himself not so much as an Impressionist but as a "realist" who adhered to and even promoted Ruskinian ideals, both in his art and in his writings. A belief in clarity of arrangement and message made the artist somewhat uncomfortable with the work of many Impressionists, particularly the French, whose "enthusiasm for color and vibration" tended, by his estimation, to neglect "values, drawings and unity in composition." For him, the soft edges of French forms came at the expense of "truth" and disrupted the harmony of the result.[24]

Although Payne celebrated pigment for its own sake, he questioned whether it should become a painting's primary subject, concurring with Lannie Haynes Martin's view of the Southern California art on display at the 1928 Pacific Southwest Exposition in Long Beach. "Art for art's sake . . . ," she reasoned, "has become an outworn adage. Let it be art for civilization's sake, art for nature's sake and most of all art for beauty's sake and each man will find his expression in and his relation to art."[25] Yet, Payne believed, in order to "see nature in a big way" one must render a "broad impression," achievable only by organizing the composition in masses painted with large, loaded brushes. "A broad impression with little detail is an abstract of nature," he explained. "The charm of broadly painted

pictures lies in the fact that the viewer must use his imagination; he then feels the abstract impression as intended by the artist."[26]

Payne's Impressionistic manner—seemingly so spontaneous—was carefully planned. He believed strongly that the most important component in painting was thoughtfulness and that "excepting natural talent or genius, individuality in thought is, without a doubt, the greatest single factor in creative work."[27] Finished paintings began with quick sketches and then carefully realized drawings, made on a pad of sketching paper with 6B Venus pencils that the artist shortened and held like charcoal. For those infrequent instances when he changed his mind, he kept an art-gum eraser tucked in his pocket.[28] He also rendered small oils outdoors on canvases and canvas boards, typically completing two small paintings a day—one in the morning and another after lunch—and then

Sycamore Grove, n.d. Pencil on paper, 8 x 10 in.
Collection of Mr. and Mrs. Jon R. Stuart

Left: *Edgar Payne Painting in the High Sierra,*
c. 1945–1946. Film still from the documentary
Sierra Journey. Courtesy of DeRu's Fine Arts

Below: *A Lunch Stop While the Marmon Cools,*
c. 1920. Photographer unknown. Courtesy
of DeRu's Fine Arts

stacking them in his car with double-sided push-pins until they had time to dry.[29] Finding it easier to "humanize" his landscapes back in the studio, he then used these studies to transfer outlines to larger canvases, drawing first with charcoal and then filling in shadows with dark wash.[30] For reference purposes, he sometimes used photographs, but he never copied them directly.[31] It was only after his compositions had been fully conceptualized, constructed, and laid out that Payne painted with great speed and dexterity.

To be sure, Payne knew better than most how to stage a scene. It was a skill that Southern Californians, steeped as they were in the new art of motion-picture making, greatly appreciated. Certainly the visual language of popular film was inspired by the Southland's natural settings, and the movie industry was an "irresistible lodestone" for artists of the "crayon, brush and other allied crafts."[32] Scenes favored by Hollywood's artists, especially in the popular genre of the western, paralleled in vision the scenery that Payne realized on canvas, which in turn stemmed from his own work as a set painter and handyman for a theatrical troupe at age twenty. Payne's early experience in painting and rigging scenery, and occasionally joining the performance itself, served him well. So good were his backdrops, especially those he created for westerns, that audiences applauded when the curtain went up.[33] Late in his career, Payne even made a documentary film of his travels into the Sierra Nevada, in which he is shown painting and enjoying his surroundings with friends (opposite). Titled *Sierra Journey,* the film was produced in full color by Payne Pictorials and first screened in 1946. It was "a scenic picture of the rugged California mountains as seen through the artist's eyes."[34]

Southern California's good weather and seductive scenery meant that Payne, like a cameraman, could find "pictures" readily available for every sort of story imaginable. He learned to see the world in carefully orchestrated vistas, each captured as he moved from one scenic locale to another. "Though Mr. Payne has never been a mere painter of scenery, he has painted big scenes, though not in a detached and impersonal manner," wrote Antony Anderson.[35] Whereas earlier generations of California painters, working in Hudson River, Luminist, and more picturesque styles, had envisioned the world in static scenes, Payne recorded a serially changing landscape that captured fleeting moments in nature—light, color, clouds—through rhythm, movement, dynamic compositions, and expressive brushwork.[36] He also believed in providing a broad impression of the view at hand, which he "observed with eyes squinted" in order to create the necessary expansiveness and unity among disparate parts of the composition.[37]

In achieving these broad impressions, Payne certainly used his imagination, and he often sacrificed his long-held adherence to truth in favor of a more powerful composition. Although his landscapes are certainly believable, Payne took considerable artistic license in creating them, and many departed significantly from the topography and vegetation of the site depicted. He was a landscape architect of truly colossal scale and, in limited instances, a literal mover of mountains. Frequently, he would front his rugged peaks with lakes imported from other locations. He also adjusted mountain profiles to accommodate a more sweeping expanse of sky. He would sometimes bring distant peaks together in a single composition in an effort to enhance the grandiosity of the scene.[38]

Packing in the Sierra, n.d. Oil on canvas, 40 x 40 in. Collection of Bette Midler. Image courtesy of Bonhams & Butterfields

Payne's ability to record and then alter such grand vistas was attributable to the fact that he could make the first part of his journey via automobile and then hike or use pack animals to reach inaccessible locales. Previous generations of artists dependent on trains and horses to make the entire journey simply could not get to the remote areas that Payne depicted. Now, for the first time, Payne and others could take a drive to enjoy the region's abundant scenery. Journalist H. Raymond Henry called Payne's predilection for doing so a sign of his being "nomadic in spirit" and referred to Payne's lifework as a virtual travelogue.[39]

The glories of motoring through Southern California had, by Payne's time, become nationally renowned, and autoists could "travel hundreds of miles in ease and comfort through some of the most beautiful country to be found in the world."[40] By the 1920s, Los Angeles claimed one automobile for every three persons. Tourist literature and motoring magazines proliferated, and Southern Californians were urged as never before to visit the region's comely hills, canyons, and beaches. Shorter workweeks and longer vacations, which evolved during the era, allowed for such excursions. On Saturday and Sunday afternoons across the continent, highways and boulevards literally pulsed with throngs of motorists, who, according to Gustav Stickley's Arts and Crafts journal *The Craftsman,* came to find "their church and a comforting religion in God's big cathedral of the Out-of-Doors. At the end of a busy week spent in shop or office a man is hungry for just such recreation; for the dip and rise of a grass-rimmed road, for a lilt of birdsong, a brook's soft melody, the warmth of sunbeams, the fragrance of field flowers."[41] Southern California especially was at an advantage and had no shortage of places to explore. A 1921 article in the *Standard Oil Bulletin* hyped that "at a turn of the driver's wheel one may revel in scenic delights from forest to farmland, mountain to ocean, crag or wooded lake."[42] "An enumeration of the desirable subjects for the landscapist's brush in the Southwest might read like a catalogue of books on out-door themes," noted Pasadena artist and writer Frederick Roland Miner. "There would be the Mountains of the Southwest, the Cañons and Mesas, the Woods and Hills, the Shore and Sea, the Hills and Valleys, and so on."[43]

To get to his destinations, Payne early on traveled across unpaved desert roads in his Model T. He often parked in the little towns of the Owens Valley and then traveled on horseback or with mules to explore the heights of the eastern Sierra (opposite).[44] He was accompanied sometimes by a fellow artist, most often Conrad Buff, and sometimes by

Hills in California, n.d. Pencil on paper, 8 x 10 in.
Courtesy of DeRu's Fine Arts

Wooded Slopes, c. 1919–1920. Oil on canvas, 48 x 58 in. Collection of Mr. and Mrs. Alan Russak

Granite Slopes, 1920–1921. Oil on canvas, 34 x 34 in. Private collection. Courtesy of George Stern Fine Arts

students—"packers"—who were there not only to learn but also to help with equipment. Later, as roads were built and automobiles improved, trips to such places as Tioga Pass and Mammoth Lakes could be made entirely in the artist's "high-powered car," which was equipped with a large box on the running board for provisions.[45] The most inaccessible locales still required Payne to leave his automobile behind and travel with pack animals on what writer Edwin Markham described as "dim trails difficult even for a patient mule."[46] Although finding these obscure trails and climbing to high altitudes could certainly be dangerous, it was also exhilarating.

As Payne's landscape painting progressed, he came to believe that the higher and more remote the locale the better. His favorite setting was the Big Pine Lakes region, which included some of the Sierra's most towering and rugged slopes. Although the preference among Impressionists internationally was for domesticated landscapes over wilderness and for visual sensation over religious message, this was not the case for Payne and several of his Southern California colleagues, including Wendt, Braun, and Hanson Puthuff, each of whom recognized and depicted the divine presence of the Creator in the mountains. Payne loved the outdoors and was determined to rediscover a broad and epic landscape that captured and conveyed what he called the "unspeakably sublime."[47] In so doing, he, more than any other California artist of his era, made an extended study of the lakes, cascades, crags, cliffs, and glaciers of the eastern Sierra.[48] Frederick Miner described such places, where one might "climb to the heights of a new Olympus, and get close to the stars," as the "Land of Heart's Desire."[49] Payne's resolve was decidedly different from that of most artists in Europe and the East, whose

Impressionist forays into light for its own sake, genteel pursuits, urban comforts, and flowers seemed to him effete and pusillanimous. By turning to a wilder nature, he rejected refinements in favor of more vital landscape subjects instilled with force and active dynamism. Edwin Markham summarized the California that Payne sought to discover when he wrote, "I have been picturing the softer paths of California, 'with roses all the way.' But if, like Ulysses, you weary of lotus-land, where it seems always afternoon, you have only to dart out to the shores or fly into the Sierras to find nature still wild and elemental."[50] Payne wanted to translate such qualities into his paintings; in the eyes of his critics and patrons, he succeeded. Many of the era described Payne's work as masculine, vigorous, and spiritual. Critic Fred Hogue even compared Payne's accomplishments to those of God himself. "The artist is transformed into the god of the mountains," he proclaimed. "He creates them, models them, and adorns them, even as the creator of the heavens and the earth."[51]

Certainly the reverential Payne found God in the landscape and in the mystical light and color he set down in flickering strokes. "The necromancy of noonday light holds a fascination for the landscape painter that he cannot escape," described an early biographer. "He is forever trying to perform the same magic on canvas."[52] In California, Payne was certainly not alone in his reverence, for a common artistic and intellectual thread in landscape painting in the early years of the twentieth century was a belief in divinity having been bestowed upon the American wilderness. In Southern California, Payne shared such intuitions with colleagues, most notably Braun, Puthuff, and Wendt, but artistic and literary figures throughout

Untitled [Landscape with Distant Mountains], n.d. Oil on canvas, 24 x 28 in. Courtesy of The Irvine Museum

Capistrano Canyon, n.d. Oil on canvas, 28 x 34 in. Private collection. Courtesy of The Irvine Museum

EDGAR PAYNE

the state espoused similar views. These had initially been popularized in New England in the first half of the nineteenth century by Transcendentalist pioneers: Thomas Carlyle, Ralph Waldo Emerson, and Henry David Thoreau. Like these writers, many Californians came to believe that the landscape manifested the Divine. "Commercialism was not the motive for the settlement on this sacred soil," argued Agnes Elding Pallen, a writer for the *Los Angeles Times*. "No!—her roots sink deeper. Her backbone is religion, coupled with the love of nature."[53]

Transcendentalism's essential tenets—a belief in the eternity of the land, the oneness of nature and the Divine, and the omnipresence of God and God's manifestation through light—were particularly apropos for California artists living amid glorious scenery. "Payne is a lover of the mountains," journalist Fred Hogue explained. "He was born in their purple shadows and every summer for the last ten years he has spent in silent, solitary communion with the everlasting hills."[54] Writer Caroline Walker detected a similar "ominous peace" in Payne's work, sensing in the vast silences of his canvases "the thing which a human soul feels in the still places where 'man is so near to the power that men call God that he ceases for a moment to breathe in the mountains [sic] fastness lest he shall hear Him lean down and whisper.'"[55] Payne's own daughter, Evelyn Payne Hatcher, concurred, stating that mountains had a spiritual quality for her father and that his paintings showed it.[56] She explained:

> I have always felt that landscape had to
> him a deeper meaning than just a direct
> representation of a place. I was very interested
> to read recently that in the American tradition

A View of the Glacial Path, n.d. Oil on canvas, 40 x 50 in. Payton Family Collection. Image courtesy of Redfern Gallery

landscape took on a mystical religious quality which in Europe was more often portrayed by human figures, and that the sense of transcendental expressed through nature and portrayed in artistic form in landscape was a real tradition. Now I never heard my father say anything like this; certainly he never mentioned the transcendental qualities of landscape—he would be more likely to say "Hm-m-m, nice," but when I read this I had a sense of tremendous familiarity, because I sense that this was indeed his feeling, and much of the small figure in the large world conveyed to me very strongly the sense of not merely respect for nature, but a feeling towards the divine.[57]

Transcendentalism was particularly strong in the American West in part because of the influence of John Muir, defender of the Sierra wilderness. On his mantel, Muir displayed portraits of Emerson and Thoreau, and like them he recognized the landscape (in his case the California wilderness) as God's handi-work. Muir's thoughts on the landscape were highly influential, especially to artists and thinkers around California, who needed only to look at the grand mountains and golden hillsides, the miles of Pacific coastline, and the density and diversity of flora to find truth in his ideas. California light especially seemed an extension of the hand of the "Master Colorist—of Him who displays his delight in wondrous color."[58] The immensity of the landscape also inspired devotion and fostered a feeling of "smallness" in the face of its Promethean scope. Muir, though he greatly admired Thoreau, mocked the author's notion that anything

"wild" could be found in the area around Concord, Massachusetts. "Wilderness," the word he used in his own writing, was embodied in the majesty of the Sierra, not in New England.[59] Payne certainly agreed with this assessment and broadened Muir's view even further to include Europe, finding the mountains there "tame, domesticated, colorless, compared to the wild vastness of the Sierras of California."[60]

Others too found something raw and visceral in California's wilderness, and it was in capturing this physical power that Payne would ultimately earn his reputation. Frank Norris's book *McTeague: A Story of San Francisco* (1899) described the primal forces of the Sierra in Northern California, which with exacting detail paralleled the setting that Payne ultimately dis-covered and made famous in the Southland:

At turns of the road, on the higher points, cañons disclosed themselves far away, gigantic grooves in the landscape, deep blue in the distance, opening one into another, ocean-deep, silent, huge, and suggestive of colossal primeval forces held in reserve. At their bottoms they were solid, massive; on their crests they broke delicately into fine serrated edges where the pines and redwoods outlined their million of tops against the high white horizon. Here and there the mountains lifted themselves out of the narrow river beds in groups like giant lions rearing their heads after drinking. The entire region was untamed. In some places east of the Mississippi nature is cosy, intimate, small, and homelike, like a good-natured housewife. In Placer County, California, she is a vast, unconquered brute of the Pliocene epoch, savage, sullen, and magnificently indifferent to man.[61]

Payne's paintings and his own prose echo the writings of Transcendentalists. Thoreau's "simplicity, simplicity, simplicity" reverberates throughout Payne's writing, particularly in his conviction that artists should achieve breadth through simplicity of composition and message.[62] In his 1941 book *Composition of Outdoor Painting,* Payne explained that "all painters of note realize the importance of simplicity in composition; the subordination of detail."[63] The simplicity he sought and secured, however, was not easily achieved but was based on a thorough knowledge of his subject. His daughter recalled, "The details he studied so carefully are rarely found worked out in finished oil paintings, but he knew what he was simplifying. I was always taught," she explained, "that whatever was simplified, changed or distorted for esthetic effect, had to rest on a knowledge of the actual structure, which is best learned by drawing."[64] Emerson too prefigured Payne's conceptions, for when the author beheld a landscape, he wondered "why all thought of multitude is lost in a tranquil sense of unity."[65] Payne spoke and wrote often of the need to unify his compositions, believing firmly that pictorial unity and fine painting were absolutely "one and the same thing."[66]

BLUING AND POKEBERRY JUICE:
THE EARLY YEARS

Although Payne came ultimately to an intimate understanding of the California landscape, he did not actually visit the state until 1909, when he was twenty-six years old. On that early trip, he spent several months painting in Laguna Beach before venturing north to San Francisco. The works he produced were typically small and painterly, like *Early Fall Trees* (p. 46), a landscape with golden, sun-dappled foliage and a complementary purple hill looming in the distance.

By the time of this first trip, Payne had already traveled widely, having left home in his late teens to escape a disapproving father. Both of his parents, John Hill Payne and Nancy Ellen Reed Payne, were practical folk from Virginia who settled in the Ozarks, first in Eureka Springs, Arkansas, and then near Cassville, Missouri. Edgar was their second child, the first son among eight children, two girls and six boys, all of whom were required to tend the farm and help their father, a carpenter, as soon as they were able.[67] Chores took precedence over education, and Payne's formal schooling ended in the fifth grade, when the family returned to Arkansas and settled in Prairie Grove. It was there that the lanky eleven-year-old made his first real attempts at painting, innovating with house paint, liquid bluing, and pokeberry juice. Punished for wasting time, he ran away from home, though he quickly returned because of hunger and a case of the measles. He soon ran away again, taking a job as a janitor and painter at a boys' school in exchange for tuition and board—at least until his father retrieved him and brought him home to continue his apprenticeship in carpentry.[68] Although it was a difficult time for the young artist, this early training in woodworking would later be put to use in making frames, furniture, and boat models.

In the late summer of 1900, the Payne family moved to Lovelady, Texas. Edgar began his professional art career there by limning signs and painting scenery in the town hall. He also portrayed the battleship USS *Maine* for a high school in Conroe, Texas. Shortly thereafter, he left home for good. He lettered signs and accepted random painting assignments until 1903, when he joined a traveling theatrical troupe and painted scenery. Ultimately, he settled in Houston with his sisters,

Early Fall Trees (detail), c. 1909. Oil on cardboard, 11¾ x 13¾ in. Collection of the Frederick R. Weisman Art Museum at the University of Minnesota, Minneapolis. Gift of Evelyn Payne Hatcher, 1980.17.11

earning a living painting houses, hanging wallpaper, and working at a scene-painting shop. His experience at the latter proved career worthy, and in 1906 he partnered in establishing Payne-Morris Studios in Dallas.[69]

Payne's next move was to Chicago, where on April 1, 1907, he enrolled in a portrait-painting class at the Art Institute of Chicago. He disliked the formality of the classroom and dropped out after just two weeks. He even debated abandoning art altogether until he "discovered that nature herself was the best guide and instructor for him."[70] While landscape painting increasingly occupied his attention, his regular income came from scene and mural painting. Occasionally, sales of small easel pictures bolstered his coffers and confidence. Having become a member of the Palette & Chisel Club, he exhibited and sold through the club's displays, which were held at its headquarters in the old Athenaeum Building on Van Buren Street in Chicago. Although he remained largely self-taught, he gratefully accepted informal critiques provided by fellow Chicago artists Ralph Clarkson and Charles Francis Browne.[71]

California Musings

On his first California trip, in 1909, Payne met Elsie Palmer, an established commercial artist, in San Francisco. Palmer's father's family bred fine horses; her mother's family made jewelry and clocks. Palmer (1884–1971) had spent most of her childhood in Oakland but moved to San Francisco in 1899 following her father's death. For two years she studied at Best's Art School under Alice Best, whose husband, Arthur William Best, established the San Francisco school with his brother, Harry Cassie Best.

Palmer's meeting with Payne was arranged by a mutual friend from Chicago, artist Gordon St. Clair, to whom Palmer was informally engaged. Payne was taken with the pretty, fair-haired artist, and in the course of his three-day visit he managed to take her sketching and to dine at her family's home. Palmer was less enamored, especially of Payne's work and color sense, which she found "dull." St. Clair, who understood Payne's potential and went on to write articles about his friend, explained, "To your California bred eyes, I guess his colors *are* dull. He's used to these silvery tones around Chicago. But don't worry, he'll get it."[72]

The transformation did not take long. After encountering the West, Payne began to exploit the possibilities of California's sunshine, atmosphere, and terrain, thus distancing his work from that of other Chicago painters. Antony Anderson explained later that "at first our tremendous scale of light bothered the Chicago painter somewhat, for he was accustomed to the mists from Michigan, but when he got his bearings . . . he began to paint strong and colorful things that show he understood California scenery and southern light."[73]

Payne–Morris Studios: Payne and Morris Scene Painting, early 1900s. Photographer unknown. Courtesy of DeRu's Fine Arts

Above: *Eucalypti*, n.d. Pencil on paper, 11 x 8½ in.
Collection of Mr. and Mrs. Jon R. Stuart

Right: *Untitled [Eucalypti]*, n.d. Oil on canvas, 28 x 32 in.
Collection of Reed and Chris Halladay

Palmer went to Chicago to see St. Clair soon thereafter and was offered a job by the Thomas Cusack Company, then the nation's leading outdoor advertising firm. She decided to stay. In 1911, she received a better offer from Clague Advertising and went to work there.[74] That same year, Payne made another visit to California and spent four months scene painting in Edwin Flagg's Los Angeles studio. He returned to Chicago with a variety of California sketches, intending to develop them into paintings. He also pursued Palmer, who by then was no longer engaged. Their courtship culminated in a Chicago wedding on November 9, 1912, after which the bride joined her husband in the affordable Tree Studio Building on East Ohio Street.

Payne had been painting murals and pursuing other decorative work with Henry Kratzner in the Payne-Kratzner Studios. He also exhibited with the Chicago Palette & Chisel Club and took part in group exhibitions at the Art Institute of Chicago. His 1911 excursion to California included a summer trip to Santa Catalina Island, Laguna Canyon, and Laguna Beach, where he painted "a few very vigorous long-shore sketches," an unusual choice for a midwestern artist unaccustomed to such subject matter. "Though he disclaims any great familiarity with the sea," Antony Anderson explained, "and rather decries his few efforts at picturing its evanescent moods, I liked his 'Low Tide' and 'The Little Cove' immensely."[75] Payne was, at times, accompanied by friends on these sketching excursions and learned from their example. One was watercolorist Norman St. Clair; another was Hanson Puthuff, who Payne knew from the Palette & Chisel Club. Puthuff's sparkling light and mountainous subject matter certainly influenced Payne's own efforts (opposite, p. 52).

Back in Chicago, Payne contributed fresh works to group exhibitions of Chicago artists at the Art Institute and to shows organized by the Palette & Chisel Club. The paintings included California views such as *The Patriarch of the Canyon, Shadows in the Canyon,* and *The Bay of Avalon* (p. 53).[76] At the same time, he

Above left: *The Paynes in Santa Barbara,* 1915. Photographer unknown. Courtesy of DeRu's Fine Arts

Above right: *Logo for Studio of Edgar Payne and Elsie Payne,* n.d. Courtesy of DeRu's Fine Arts

continued to paint murals and decorations for court-houses and theaters, now often working in partnership with Elsie, who frequently painted figures in her husband's landscapes. Projects included the Northern Hotel in Billings, Montana; the Queen Theater in Houston, Texas; and the Empress Theatre in Chicago. In 1913, Payne also became a member of the Union internationale des beaux-arts et des lettres in Paris.

That same year, Payne exhibited sixty-five "vivid and glowing studies of the hills and canyons of California" with the Palette & Chisel Club.[77] The exhibition sold out, and he spent the proceeds on another sketching trip to California with Elsie. They stayed through the summer, and in the fall they returned to Chicago, where on January 12, 1914, their daughter, Evelyn (p. 50), was born. With a growing family and increasing expenses, Payne was reluctant to give up profitable

mural painting, and that year he fulfilled a commission from the Mitchell and Holbeck Company of Chicago for the Hendricks County Courthouse in Danville, Indiana. He also completed murals on the themes of mercy and justice for the Clay County Courthouse in Brazil, Indiana, and a survey of paintings depicting American history for the American Theater in Chicago. The latter was an enormous project, to which Elsie lent her figurative skills for various expedition and battle scenes; Edgar concentrated on a sixty-foot allegorical mural, titled *Progress*, over the proscenium arch and a mountainous landscape on the drop curtain.

Also in 1914, Payne exhibited at the Art Institute of Chicago and held a joint exhibition with sculptor Nancy Cox-McCormack at the Palette & Chisel Club headquarters. His major exhibition of the following year took place in San Francisco at the Panama-Pacific

Hanson Puthuff (American, 1875–1972). *Mystical Hills*, n.d. Oil on canvas, 26 x 34 in.
Courtesy of The Irvine Museum

Canyon Mission Viejo, Capistrano, n.d. Oil on canvas, 24 x 28 in. Private collection. Courtesy of The Irvine Museum

The Bay of Avalon, 1911. Oil on canvas, 33 x 42 in. The Edward H. and Yvonne J. Boseker Collection. Image courtesy of DeRu's Fine Arts

International Exposition, where he showed and later sold a mountainscape, *Infinitude,* in the arts section and a painting titled *Dewy Eve* in the Illinois State Building. The Paynes traveled to San Francisco to see the entries firsthand and to visit Elsie's family.

The Paynes spent the rest of the summer in Santa Barbara and while there made an excursion to Santa Cruz Island, one of the Channel Islands just off the coast (p. 56). The islands' natural caves, particularly Cueva Valdez on Santa Cruz Island's north shore, encouraged Edgar's long fascination with maritime subjects and pirating and resulted in a series of photographs, sketches, and paintings. Some paintings, such as *The Sea Rovers* and *The Buccaneers,* feature close-up views of picturesque pirates on a fateful dark blue ocean. These not only were "full of dramatic suggestion" but also showcased Payne's ability to paint the human figure.[78] Others prioritized the setting. Permeated with color, *The Rendezvous (Santa Cruz Island, CA)* (opposite) depicts an opalescent blue-green sea and the golden, vortexlike cliff of Cueva Valdez, which swirls around a group of pirates camped at the cave's eastern entrance.

Having "read a lot about pirates," Payne had been awaiting just such an opportunity.[79] He was intimately familiar with Robert Louis Stevenson's famous *Treasure Island* (1883) and also with Howard Pyle's pirate illustrations and writings, which would ultimately be assembled in Pyle's posthumously published *Book of Pirates* (1921).[80] Stevenson's writings in particular thrilled Payne's imagination with their swashbuckling ruffians who plied the seas and pillaged exotic locales. Like Stevenson, who recalled the rugged shoreline of the Monterey Peninsula for *Treasure Island*'s dramatic landscape descriptions, Payne found inspiration in California's vigorous coast.

The Rendezvous (Santa Cruz Island, CA), 1915.
Oil on canvas, 33 x 42 in. Private collection

In reality, the pirates in Payne's paintings were the artist, his wife, and their fellow Chicago painter and frame maker O. Irwin Myers, who had joined the excursion and took turns posing in a rented costume (below right).[81] While on the island, Payne made dozens of sketches and photographs, which proved well worth the effort—at least when the action remained incidental to the landscape. Critics and viewers regarded *The Rendezvous* highly when Payne exhibited it in 1916 at the Art Institute of Chicago and

with the Palette & Chisel Club, of which he was then a leading member. Reception of the figurative pieces, however, was mixed. When these paintings were exhibited a second time in Chicago, at the Moulton and Ricketts Art Galleries, critic Albrecht Montgelas decided that he "would have rather not again seen those paintings of fantastic looking pirates," which he found to be "illustrational in character as well as in execution."[82]

Above left: *Sketching on Santa Cruz Island,* 1915. Photographer unknown. Courtesy of DeRu's Fine Arts

Above right: *Edgar Payne in Pirate Costume,* 1915. Photographer unknown. Courtesy of DeRu's Fine Arts

EPIC CADENCES

As is evident in *The Rendezvous,* Payne's once tranquil style was becoming increasingly tumultuous, which seemed to mirror the conflict and unrest of the world at large. World War I was raging in Europe, and soon the United States would become officially involved. The country was permeated with a great deal of anxiety, to which the Paynes and other artists were certainly not immune. Northern California art critic Laura Bride Powers described an emerging need among artists of the era for color, which to her seemed an antidote to dark times. "It is splendid," she wrote, "the cry for color all over the world, at a time when there's so much drab in it."[83]

For Payne, the war would ultimately have direct and personal connections. On September 7, 1918, he registered for the draft in Orange County, California. Although Payne himself never served, his brother Alonzo saw active duty and was wounded. Because Alonzo did not come home until 1926, his family believed for years that he had died at the front. Payne also went so far as to write an essay on world peace, asking how, at a time when it was "the most important thought and the most fervent wish, in the minds of everyone," it might be achieved.[84] Elsie did her part as an active volunteer with the Red Cross.

Payne made the California coast manifest his apprehensions of the world at large. He admitted that

William Ritschel (American, b. Germany, 1864–1949). *The Instealing Fog,* 1916. Oil on canvas, 50 x 60 in. Crocker Art Museum. Gift of the Ladies Museum Association, 1939.61.1

there was more to his paintings than met the eye, and he believed firmly that each work should incorporate a "quality that exhilarates and lifts the mind beyond the mere making of a picture."[85] Certainly the many coastal scenes he painted during this period echoed war's ominous voice in their pounding tides. He and other California artists of the war era, most notably William Ritschel and Armin Hansen of the Monterey Peninsula region, moved their work away from the quiet, still styles of the previous generation and toward an active, restless dynamism exemplified by the Pacific shore (p. 57).[86] Payne in particular felt that the artist needed to express "attributes which are beyond vision." "The power is given to him to feel," he said, "the mystery and charm of fleeting clouds; the immensity and depth of blue skies and atmospheric distances; the grace and rhythm of living and expanding trees and other growths; the nobility, grandeur and strength of mighty peaks; the endless movement and vitality of the sea and its forms."[87] California's rocky coastline admirably suited this pursuit. Antony Anderson noted that the Laguna coast in particular forced artists to "wrestle with a great nature" because there "the iron backbone of the world shows in the ridges of rocks that lift themselves above the angry protests of the sea."[88]

In his book *Composition of Outdoor Painting,* Payne identified a fundamental quality of his art. "At the basis of all things there is energy, activity or power—call it what you will," he explained, "that is produced between opposing forces."[89] This he aimed to capture in his vigorous Laguna marines by featuring the vitality of the Pacific's endless struggle against the rocky shore, not just the beauty of light and color for their own sake. Payne's seascapes suggest an affinity with paintings by the American painter Winslow Homer, who produced a series of works featuring the Maine coast, many of which depict only restless water, shoreline, and sky. A strong advocate of studying the work of others before finding one's own originality, Payne did not deny Homer's influence.[90] Furthermore, he believed that the artistry of a great painter is tested by the painter's success in interpreting the active and violent moods of the ocean.[91] Antony Anderson agreed, finding a deeply personal expression in Payne's paintings of the Pacific and stating that Payne sang his tune in "epic cadences" by preferring the boisterous and ever-changing moods of the forceful sea.[92] It was a predilection that the critic found well suited to the artist's abilities and one worth continuing. "There are plenty of other painters who can give us, in exquisite perfection, the ocean's apolescent [*sic*] tranquility," he reasoned.[93]

In late 1916, Payne painted *Restless Sea* (p. 60), which he completed in his Chicago studio from sketches made at Laguna Beach. A churning, dynamic composition of the ocean and rocky coast, it features a battle between rocks and sea under a sunset sky. A far cry from the artist's placid Laguna marines produced earlier in the decade, the painting must have been particularly poignant when Payne exhibited it at the Art Institute of Chicago in early 1917, the

Untitled [Laguna Seascape], c. 1918. Oil on canvas, 43¹/₁₆ x 43⅛ in. Collection of D. L. Stuart Jr.

Restless Sea, 1917. Oil on canvas, 43 x 51 in. Indianapolis Museum of Art. Gift of Mrs. James Sweetser, 17.66

eve of America's entry into the war. Because it was quickly purchased, similar paintings followed. His *Angry Waters, Surging Sea, Eternal Surge* (p. 63), and *Coward's Cove* (p. 68) depict the coastal waters of Laguna Beach with elegant water patterns and swirling tides interwoven between sunlit rocks. *Sentinels of the Coast, Monterey* (p. 66) and *Monterey Cypress* (p. 67) depict windblown cypresses from the Monterey Peninsula, farther north, which cling to the rocky shore in a battle for survival. Other coastals, such as *Summer Sea,* incorporate flying gulls, distant breakers, and large clouds.[94] *Silver Light* features rocks and turbulent waves. *Deep Sea,* in reductive simplicity, includes nothing but sky and blue-green waves, as does his small but animated *Rhythmic Sea,* which eliminates the coast entirely to show only breaking waves under a cloudy sky. The latter in particular is a visual manifestation of the artist's belief in an underlying rhythm in nature, of which he frequently spoke and wrote. "To feel the spirit of nature is to feel the rhythmic, spiritual flow which encircles animate and inanimate nature," Payne wrote, "the rhythm of life and the universe."[95]

Payne was certainly not the first artist or writer to analogize war with California's restive coastal waters. Just two years earlier, Edwin Markham had written in *California the Wonderful* of a "rallying place of waves" near Point San Pedro in San Pablo Bay. "Twelve feet high, the mile-long columns advance with greatening volume, a charge of Neptune's white-maned cavalry, rushing in thunder on the waiting shores—ever defeated, crushed and broken, ever regathering their shattered squadrons for a new assault on the impossible."[96] Markham also beheld a similar stretch of wild coast in the south, at La Jolla,

where "since the youth of the world, the cliffs and the sea have waged eternal battle."[97] Robert Louis Stevenson had earlier found such a site on the Monterey Peninsula, where "even in quiet weather, the low, distant, thrilling roar of the Pacific hangs over the coast and the adjacent country like smoke above a battle."[98]

The broad, universal, and age-old theme of nature, its contests, and man's small place within it was similarly described in verse by Robinson Jeffers, who moved to Carmel in 1914 after living in Los Angeles. Jeffers's poetry, like Payne's paintings, frequently portrayed the powerful forces of California nature as well as the enduring struggle between land and sea. The rhythmic, rugged splendor of his poems corresponded in conception and date not only to Payne's paintings but also to those of other California progressives of his generation—such as Hansen and Ritschel. The poet's descriptions of the coastal landscape, the feeling of "ocean pounding granite," were imbued with a new century's sense of turmoil, violence, and fierce monumentality.[99] "The ocean swelled for a far storm and beat its boundary, the ground-swell shook the beds of granite," Jeffers wrote.[100] Surely Payne's realization of these metaphoric possibilities was no coincidence, for at the end of the Great War, works such as *Restless Sea* gave way briefly to landscapes filled with joyful "pastel tints." The uncharacteristic transition in palette and mood did not go unnoticed by the press and seemed to symbolize the artist's new hope and optimism for the world.[101]

Untitled [Laguna Coastal Scene], n.d. Oil on canvas, 33 x 42 in. Crocker Art Museum. Gift of Mrs. Charles G. Johnson, conserved with funds provided by the Historical Collections Council of California Art

Eternal Surge, c. 1920. Oil on canvas, 34 x 54 in. Laguna Art Museum Collection. Museum Purchase with funds from prior gift of Louis Outerbridge, 2002.009

Laguna Coastline, n.d. Oil on canvas, 28 x 34 in. Private collection.
Courtesy of William A. Karges Fine Arts

Sentinels of the Coast, Monterey, 1921. Oil on canvas, 28 x 34 in. Courtesy of The Irvine Museum

Monterey Cypress, c. 1921. Oil on canvas, 15 x 18 in. Barnett Family Collection

Coward's Cove, 1916. Oil on canvas on Masonite, 36 x 44 in. Private collection. Courtesy of Redfern Gallery

DRAMA OF MAGNIFICENCE

Rejecting the tranquil gentility of the previous generation, Payne began his excursions into the wild and elemental at the coast. Ultimately, however, he moved inland to the highest, most remote regions of the Sierra Nevada, which, according to the artist's daughter, he loved above all other mountains.[102] With the United States embroiled in the war, he made his first of many trips in 1917 or 1918, camping and finding inspiration for paintings that emanate spiritual power and force. Juxtaposing the weight and mass of the majestic peaks against crystalline lakes, his depictions of these mountains were meant not to imitate nature but to interpret it, yet most critics agreed that no artist in California could capture the Sierra with "greater fidelity to nature than he."[103] Ultimately, these paintings would garner him the moniker "the God of the Mountains," and a lake in the headwaters of Piute Canyon would come to bear his name.[104]

The virility of these subjects, along with similar scenes depicted by other artists, was perceived as ruggedly American, particularly during the war years, when artists, tastemakers, and even politicians encouraged the pursuit of a regional "Americanness." Writer Michael Williams described this "virile Americanism" as the dominant note of the 1915 Panama-Pacific International Exposition. "I affirm this quality," he said. "I dare to assert that it is the most American thing that has happened in art on this western continent."[105] Former president Theodore Roosevelt agreed, bellowing at a joint meeting of the American Academy of Arts and Letters and the National Institute of Arts and Letters in 1916 that "American work must smack of our own soil, mental and moral, no less than physical, or it will have little of permanent value," and it should "express the distinctive characteristics of our own national soul."[106] Payne did his best to follow this advice and began to self-consciously identify himself as just such an American painter, especially in his Sierra subjects. His message was clearly received. "He's an individualist, and an American—even a Westerner," Antony Anderson contended, "and his native spots are always there."[107]

For many, the West itself was "the most American part of America," at least according to English traveler and writer James Bryce—"the part where those features which distinguish America from Europe come

Payne Lake and the Artist with Cairn, n.d. Photographer unknown. Courtesy of DeRu's Fine Arts

Sierra Peaks, c. 1919. Oil on canvas, 42 x 42 in. Collection of D. L. Stuart Jr.

out in the strongest relief."[108] New York painter and teacher Robert Henri agreed, writing in 1914 that "the new Western school of painting will not be an imitation of all the others that have gone before it, but will be strongly individual, inimitably of the big free West. You have the opportunity here to advance in your own way because you are happily removed from any large center of conservative traditions. Compelled to blaze your own trail, you will grow fearless and strong."[109] This seemed to apply specifically to Payne, whose love of country and quintessential western Americanism was compared to that of artists Frederic Remington and Charles Russell. One Illinois writer found that Payne "re-created for mankind the handiwork of the Great Being in his happiest moods," just as Remington and Russell had preserved the "vanishing types of the great west."[110]

In showcasing the glories of California to its citizens and the nation at large, Payne avoided quintessential—and in his mind overused—Northern California subjects such as the Yosemite Valley, Mount Shasta, and Mount Tamalpais. He sought "new" settings in the Southland that were dramatic and *big,* bringing greater attention to less explored natural glories. Fortunately for Payne, the local landscape admirably suited his purposes. "Again and again in California great Nature, the mystic world-mother, has sounded the note sublime," wrote the poet Edwin Markham. "Seashore, desert, mountain, giant tree, strange valley, towering cliff—all have been staged for a world spectacle, a drama of magnificence."[111] Although Payne certainly tried his hand at all of these subjects, for journalist Arthur Millier it was the southern Sierra pictures that brought the most pleasure. "'Peaks Sublime' shows Payne at his full powers as a mountain painter," Millier

wrote. "Here he realizes the weight and mass of huge mountains and the comparative simplicity of his technique aids the impression of grandeur."[112] "Mr. Payne sees nature in a big and impressive way," affirmed Anderson, "and something of this bigness of outlook he communicates to us."[113]

Payne was absolutely convinced that the Sierra Nevada possessed a greater appeal to the lover of nature, the romantic, the beautiful, and the sublime than did the mountains of any other country, even though he had painted ranges throughout Europe. "No artist in my newspaper career has brought home to me how little we appreciate our own country like Edgar Alwyn [*sic*] Payne," wrote Fred Hogue. "I wonder if even those who have been preaching to us 'see America first' have appreciated what marvels

Sierra Peak, n.d. Pencil on paper, 8 x 9 in. Collection of John and Judith Ibbetson

Near Sabrina, n.d. Oil on canvas, 20 x 24 in. Collection of Mr. John Mutch. Courtesy of Redfern Gallery

there are in our own country to see."[114] With equal "patriotic fervor," writer Sonia Wolfson of the *California Graphic* turned from Payne's paintings of the Alps to his scenes of the Sierra and then breathed an "unconscious prayer of thanksgiving for the beauties of . . . homeland and the artists who, knowing the glories of other lands, are big enough to convey them."[115] Even Payne's European scenes, which he showed at Chicago's Newcomb Macklin & Co. in the spring of 1925, were thought by one reporter to be "very American in character. There is a bigness, a feeling for the sweep of space, a grasp of fundamental features and an absence of unessential detail that mark the work of the great American landscape painters."[116]

Also motivating Payne was the sense of urgency that he felt in recording the pristine beauty of the Sierra. The "feeling of communion with nature" that he readily experienced in California, for instance, had been mitigated in the Swiss Alps by development. "Even on the peaks, one finds there shelter huts," Payne reported. "The slopes are cultivated to the snow line. The hotels follow you everywhere."[117] He feared the same thing happening at home as the housing, factories, refineries, and power plants that were already part of the Los Angeles landscape spilled into outlying areas. As early as 1902, California author Frank Norris had declared that there was "no longer any Frontier," yet this was only the beginning of the "steady march of civilization" that was to come.[118] In 1900, Los Angeles's population was just 100,000, but by 1920, it approached 600,000, a growth accommodated by the Owens Valley aqueduct, which imported water into the city. Payne's beloved nature—and by extension the divinity present therein—was

fast succumbing to "progress," urban sprawl, and industry. Fred Hogue lamented:

> A score of landscapists and genre painters are writing the contemporary history of the first half of the twentieth century in Southern California. The groves they paint will disappear. The Laguna of today will not be that of tomorrow. The encroachments of trade and commerce will destroy the primitive beauty of some of the enchanted spots in the Southland; and the generations which come after will turn to these canvases as the records of a departed epoch.
>
> Progress, in some of its manifestations is deadly to art. It is a motor tank that, to reach its objective, crushes ruthlessly, unknowingly all that lies in its path . . .
>
> Only the snowmantled mountain peaks resist the encroachments of a money-mad generation. They show no scars of the passage of the hosts of civilization, the defilers of beauty.[119]

Payne, therefore, like other artists, aimed to preserve what he could of California's beauty—on canvas if not in reality. The Sierra scenes that he chose to depict were thus an escape from industrialization, development, and a burgeoning population. He portrayed not California's rapidly changing built environment but the unpopulated and untrammeled Eden of pure nature and wilderness. He also tried to live his aesthetic by communing with nature as often as possible. He was certainly not alone in this, for Californians, more than residents of any other state in the nation, enjoyed a special bond with the outdoors and embraced nature and its healthful attributes as never before. This "back-to-nature movement" stressed the virtues of fresh air,

The Topmost Sierra, c. 1921. Oil on canvas, 43 x 43 in. W. C. Foxley Collection

Timber Line, n.d. Oil on canvas, 20 x 24 in. Collection of Linda and Jim Freund

Pack Train in the High Sierra, 1930s. Oil on canvas, 30 x 40 in. Collection of Gilbert and Nancy Waldman. Courtesy of John R. Howard Fine Art

living in the open, and a strenuous life, and the higher one went, the greater the potential benefit.[120] Many sought the restorative aspects of scaling mountains and breathing the thin air of high altitudes. George Wharton James urged readers to "get into the open, climb the heights, brave the storms, if you would become strong, if you would beget powerful sons and beautiful daughters, if you would live, triumph, and endure."[121] Edwin Markham found realms of untainted purity in the highest elevations of the Sierra. "There is health on those levels for my sore afflicted brothers locked up in cities," he wrote, "cisterns of pure untainted air, kingdoms of rest and silence."[122] Writer Mary Austin recognized it too, but in the upper reaches of the desert—places where one could find the "divinest, cleanest air to be breathed anywhere in God's world. Some day the world will understand that," she continued, "and the little oases on the windy tops of hills will harbor for healing its ailing, house-weary broods."[123] Yet even by these standards, the remoteness and duration of Payne's excursions into the vastness of the Sierra far exceeded the travels of most Californians. He depicted the highest locales with the clearest water, the most unblemished terrain, and the purest, most ultracrystalline light as if he were recording these settings for posterity.

At home, Payne tried to bring nature indoors through an abundance of wood, objects, and outdoor motifs. His rustic Arts and Crafts studio in Laguna Beach included hand-carved furniture that he made, rugs that Elsie wove, and Native American pottery, both for use and for decoration. A snakeskin hung on the wall, and a bearskin rug fronted a fieldstone fireplace.[124] Like these collected bits of nature, Payne's paintings offered an oasis of tranquility. In

his *Composition of Outdoor Painting,* he quoted Sir John Gilbert calling paintings "loopholes of escape to the soul . . . , where the fancy for a moment may revel, refreshed and delighted. Pictures are consolers of loneliness, and a relief to the jaded mind, and windows to the imprisoned thought; they are books, histories and sermons—which we can read without turning over the leaves."[125]

In part for this reason, Payne included human beings in relatively few of his California paintings, and when he did so they were typically shown in harmony with nature, a minor footprint in the landscape (opposite). Figures became a regular and integral part of Payne's compositions only in the desert Southwest. There, humanity—and Native Americans in particular—seemed at one with the environment. And there, human presence remained small and unobtrusive when set against the vast loneliness of the terrain.

LEADING A COLONY: LAGUNA BEACH

Payne's fascination with the Southwest was encouraged in 1916 when he joined and became first vice president of The Trailers, a club of painters who came together with the intention of making an eight- to ten-week painting tour of the West. The Chicago, Burlington & Quincy Railroad (known as the Burlington Route) agreed to provide club members with scenic transport and special accommodations as they visited the West's national parks and other natural wonders.[126] Payne, however, did not end up making this trip but accepted a similar assignment from the Atchison, Topeka & Santa Fe Railway Company (commonly called the Santa Fe Railway) to paint western scenery. Provided with transportation by the railroad, he arrived in Gallup, New Mexico, with his wife and young daughter on June 25, 1916. The family immediately set off by car, heading west to Ganado, Arizona, and then to the Canyon de Chelly, making their destination by nightfall. Thereafter, in order to take full advantage of the region's aesthetic opportunities, Payne rented a wagon to go from site to site.[127] For the next four months, he lived on and near Navajo and Hopi reservations and sketched and painted the spectacular scenery.

The summer following the trip, Payne moved to Glendale, California, although he continued to maintain a Chicago address until 1925. In Tropico, a neighborhood of Glendale, he rented an abandoned piano factory, which he occupied as a studio in order to fulfill a mural commission for the Congress Hotel in Chicago. The scale and financial remuneration of the commission were impressive, calling for a continuous set of murals to line the corridors of all eleven floors and staircases of the hotel, a project that would earn Payne $12,000. In order to accomplish the enormous task, which required thousands of pounds of white lead and some 11,000 square yards of canvas, Payne enlisted the help of artist friends Peter Nielsen, Jack Wilkinson Smith, and Fred Grayson Sayre. Conrad Buff later joined the team. According to Buff, Elsie kept track of the dimensions from the blueprints; Smith and Payne painted the foreground with Sayre's help; Nielsen painted garlands and flowers "all over the place"; and Buff stretched canvases and painted the sky and clouds. The project took four months of Herculean effort to complete.[128]

As he finished the murals, Payne made the decision to move to Laguna Beach, inviting his muralist colleagues to join him. He even offered Buff a job as a cook in exchange for a place to live. The group sketched during the day in good company, as Laguna Beach was fast becoming an art colony of national importance.[129] Elsie wrote of the couple's first year there:

> There was an interesting group down there that winter. The very serious Conrad Buff, the debonair Jack Wilkinson Smith—Elmer Wachtell [sic] of the sardonic wit . . . The genial William Griffith [and Frank] Cuprien the self-sufficient and picturesque. In the mainstreet was a rough wood moving picture house, an ice cream parlor, and a bowling alley under a tent. We used to all come there of evenings to bowl. Elmer Wachtell christened it "The Gilded Palace of Vice."[130]

Numerous other artists lived and painted in Laguna Beach; among the most prominent were Anna Hills, William and Julia Bracken Wendt, and Karl Yens. George Gardner Symons was also there early on, keeping a studio south of Laguna, at Arch Beach. Joseph Kleitsch and many more came shortly thereafter—some just to visit, others to live.

Payne quickly became a central figure in Laguna's art community. After renting a small cottage (opposite), he bought and extensively remodeled a shingled studio home in 1918, decorating it with motifs drawn from nature. While the house was being finished, he rented a small store for use as a studio, which later became a frame shop. Payne had made hand-carved picture frames in Chicago at The Studio Frame Shop, which he operated in partnership with Louis Grosse and O. Irwin Myers. He continued to design and carve his own Arts and Crafts–style frames in Laguna until about 1920, when he turned the business over to his apprentice, Harold "Buck" Weaver.[131]

Payne became an ardent promoter of the Laguna art scene and was instrumental in securing the old town hall as a place for artists to meet and show their work. On July 27, 1918, this new "gallery" opened its first exhibition of more than one hundred paintings and sculptures, many by premier artists of the Southland. An immediate success, the exhibition attracted 300 guests to its opening, and a total of 2,000 visited in the first three weeks.[132] A more formal organization of artists quickly proved necessary to manage the operation, and on August 15 the Paynes held a gathering in their new home that founded the Laguna Beach Art Association. Those in attendance included Roi Clarkson Colman, Frank Cuprien, Alice Fullerton, Conway Griffith, Anna Hills, Nevada Lindsay, and Ann Mason. Payne was elected the association's first president; Anna Hills became vice president. The mission of the new organization was to advance

knowledge of and interest in art and create a spirit of cooperation and fellowship between artists and the public by maintaining a permanent gallery for exhibition and sale of artists' work.[133] There were 150 founding members, 35 of whom were local artists. Within a decade, membership grew to 700 members, including 180 professional artists.[134] Exhibitions were held each month and kept to a high standard via a jury process. Artists initially took turns curating the space but later hired a staff curator.

During this same period, Payne began exhibiting with the Los Angeles–based California Art Club, which had been founded in December 1909 and held its first exhibition the following July. The organization grew out of the Painters' Club of Los Angeles (founded in 1906), which counted among its members nearly all of Southern California's premier artists, many of whom were accorded institutional

Edgar Payne's Cottage in Laguna Beach, c. 1918. Photographer unknown. Courtesy of DeRu's Fine Arts

Rugged Slopes and Tamarack, c. 1919. Oil on board, 45 x 45 in. Collection of Mr. and Mrs. Thomas B. Stiles II

recognition through the Los Angeles Museum of History, Science, and Art in Exposition Park (established in 1913). In 1919, several artists involved in the club branched into the short-lived Ten Painters' Club of California, which was organized in emulation of the East Coast's more famous group of Impressionists—the Ten American Painters. The Ten Painters' Club included Payne, Maurice Braun, Benjamin Brown, Roi Clarkson Colman, Hanson Puthuff, Guy Rose, Jack Wilkinson Smith, Elmer Wachtel, Marion Kavanagh Wachtel, and William Wendt. They exhibited together at the Kanst Art Galleries, which hung paintings by all ten artists—eight apiece—together. An adjacent gallery featured rotating solo exhibitions of members' work. An ardent supporter, J. F. Kanst advertised his stable as the "foremost painters of the West."[135]

Payne had in fact become one of the state's foremost painters, having "won fame as a painter of the sea as well as of the mountains of California."[136] His success was underscored by the medals he won at the 1918 and 1919 California State Fair art exhibitions in Sacramento and, in 1920, at the Art Institute of Chicago. The latter awarded him the coveted Martin B. Cahn Prize for the best painting by a Chicago artist at the *Thirty-Third Annual Exhibition of American Oil Paintings and Sculpture,* an honor earned for *Rugged Slopes and Tamarack* (opposite), which he had completed following his trip to the Sierra the previous summer. Nearly square in format, the painting depicts the region up the south fork of Big Pine Creek, north of Elinore Lake, in Inyo County, California. It is animated stylistically by the artist's Impressionist brushwork and compositionally by irregularly shaped patches of snow and a serpentine trail of lodgepole pines (an older common name being tamarack) that the artist

imported into the scene, which in reality is set above the timberline.[137] The artist certainly recognized the success of this painting, and he exhibited it at other venues the following year, including the Pennsylvania Academy of the Fine Arts in Philadelphia and the California Art Club at the Los Angeles Museum of History, Science, and Art.

Also in 1921, Payne exhibited in Los Angeles at the Southwest Museum's first annual exhibition of paintings by California artists. For his entry—another Sierra scene, *Topmost Crags* (pp. 82–83), which depicts peaks in the north fork of Big Pine Canyon—he won the first prize, $250. The following February, he exhibited *Solitude's Enchantment* (p. 84) at the Pennsylvania Academy of the Fine Arts in Philadelphia. From the same region as *Topmost Crags,* this painting features a southern view of the north face of Temple Crag. Payne also painted farther north, near Yosemite and Mono Lake. He was especially pleased with *Slopes of Lee Vining* (p. 85), which depicts a view of Lee Vining Creek with Tioga Peak in the center of the canvas and Gaylor Peak to the left. He valued this painting at $2,000 and exhibited it at the *Thirty-Fourth Annual Exhibition of American Oil Paintings and Sculpture* at the Art Institute of Chicago.

By late 1920, Payne had completed his term as president of the Laguna Beach Art Association and decided to move his family to Los Angeles. Early the next year, he exhibited at the newly opened Stendahl Galleries in the city's Ambassador Hotel and also showed at the gallery of O'Hara and Livermore in Pasadena and Orr's Art Gallery in San Diego. He spent much of the summer of 1921 sketching in the Sierra, and the following February he exhibited some twenty-five paintings at the Stendahl Galleries. But

Topmost Crags, 1921. Oil on canvas, 31 x 36 in. Private collection

Opposite: *Solitude's Enchantment,* 1921. Oil on canvas, 43 x 43 in. Courtesy of Edenhurst Gallery

Above: *Slopes of Lee Vining,* 1921. Oil on canvas, 48 x 58 in. Courtesy of George Stern Fine Arts

Painted place cards (clockwise from top left: *Crashing Surf, Meadow, High Sierra* verso with inscription to Alson S. Clark, *High Sierra*), presented to guests at banquet dinner hosted by the Stendahl Galleries, May 22, 1922. Oil on board, each 2¼ x 3¾ in. Collection of Jean and Linda Stern

the artist's restless nature led him to begin planning an extended trip to Europe. In a February 1922 article, Antony Anderson sang Payne's praises and announced the artist's intentions:

> Now we find him painting away for dear life
> and for months at a time in the cold and remote
> recesses of the high Sierras; now he is in the
> hottest pockets of the desert; now he is perched
> on the rocks of the Pacific. Seldom, indeed, is
> he "at home," the business of painting is too
> engrossing for that. And next summer he journeys
> to Europe, to be gone for two years in France,
> Spain, Italy and Switzerland.[138]

On May 22, 1922, on the eve of Payne's departure for Europe, the Stendahl Galleries hosted a banquet in his honor. Guests, who were thrilled to find a miniature Payne landscape at each place setting (opposite), included "artists, picture dealers, critics, museum directors, physicians, motion-picture directors and writers, picture lovers and at least one bishop."[139] Fred Hogue addressed the crowd by radio in a speech called "California the Beautiful." Los Angeles, he announced, had become the new "Athens of the Pacific," and of the art produced in the city, nothing was more noble, true, or pure than that by Edgar Payne.[140]

Carved frame for *When the Tide Is Low, Laguna Beach,* n.d. Wood, 12 x 16 in.
Collection of Simon K. Chiu

Les Haut Sierra [High Sierra], c. 1922. Oil on canvas, 43 x 43 in. Courtesy of Redfern Gallery

THE ROLLING STONE

Before he left, Payne smartly arranged to send a painting, *Silvery Light, Laguna,* to the California State Fair art exhibition in Sacramento; it won first prize that fall. The family then began their two-year journey by traveling east to Chicago. They boarded with a friend, Grace Hickox, in the Fine Arts Building on Michigan Avenue and, because Evelyn was sick, stayed there long enough for Payne to hold a brief exhibition. The Paynes finally set sail from New York in July, heading directly for Paris and remaining there through August.

The Paynes drove their Model T through the Haute-Savoie and French Alps toward Marseilles, visiting Monaco, Nice, Cannes, Antibes, and Juan-les-Pins. They spent a month in Menton, on the French Riviera, before crossing into Italy and visiting the Ligurian towns of Rapallo and Santa Margherita. They then headed for Rome. The paintings that resulted were "a splendid record" of their itinerary, which, as Antony Anderson reported, had "something of the big resonant thunder of the Odyssey Epic."[141] While wintering in Rome, Payne finished his first majestic depiction of Mont Blanc, *Le Grand Pic Blanc* (p. 116), which won an honorable mention at the 1923 Paris Salon. He also had a second painting accepted, *Les Haut Sierra [High Sierra]* (opposite). Although the painting was highly regarded, it did not win a prize.

From Rome, the Paynes traveled widely. In the early spring of 1923, they visited Tivoli, Perugia, Florence, and Genoa. In Florence, they visited the Uffizi Gallery and the Palazzo Pitti. The paintings they saw came as a pleasant surprise to Payne, who decided that "in spite of the religious subjects some of those men could *paint.*"[142] The family then headed

for Switzerland but, finding it too cold for painting, opted instead for Venice, then Chioggia.

Even while traveling, Payne maintained an extraordinary schedule of international exhibitions. That spring, he shipped twenty-six of his canvases to Los Angeles for a summer show at the Stendahl Galleries. In November, he contributed five large canvases to the *Second Biennial Roman International Exposition.* He exhibited with the American Art Association in Paris two months later and also exhibited sixteen paintings in a joint exhibition with sculptor Nancy Cox-McCormack at the Galeries Jacques Seligmann et fils. After sending his first Salon paintings, *Le Grand Pic Blanc* and *Les Haut Sierra [High Sierra],* to the Art Institute of Chicago's exhibition of Chicago artists in February 1924, he submitted two new paintings to the spring Salon. Both depicted Swiss mountains; both were accepted.

In the summer, the Paynes sketched in the Loire Valley, in Brittany, and along the Brittany coast. Before returning to the United States in 1924, they spent time in London visiting museums. Back in Chicago, where Payne spent several months, the artist showed mostly European subjects, "very American in character," in the Art Institute's exhibition of Chicago artists and at the galleries of Newcomb Macklin & Co.[143] Accompanied by George Hurrell, future Hollywood photographer, the family finally drove back to California in the spring of 1925. Payne was glad to be home. With a renewed respect for his own nationality and abilities, he declared that there was nothing in European painting that could induce him to "imitate any ism or creed."[144]

The California art community was equally pleased by Payne's return, and the *Los Angeles Times* reported that after three short and busy years in France, Italy, and Switzerland, he was "bringing with him a carload of canvases."[145] A few bemoaned the fact that Payne had left California at all. "As I studied the canvases in the present collection, I sensed a feeling of regret that he should have wandered so far," lamented Fred Hogue. "I wished he might have been imprisoned in California, like a bird in a golden cage, that he might have remained as loyal to us as the Flemish painters to the Low Countries and the British painters of the epoch of Gainsborough and Lawrence to the British Isles."[146] The Payne family spent the first part of summer at Laguna Beach, staying with their old friend Buck Weaver. In July they went north, visiting San Francisco and then the Sierra Nevada. They may also have made a short trip to Thoreau, New Mexico.

In exhibitions, Payne received awards and accolades as never before. In the summer of 1925, he took home a prize from the Laguna Beach Art Association for *Tuna Fisherman, Concarneau* (p. 154). He was awarded a gold medal for best landscape by the California Art Club for *Peaks and Shadows,* and he won the California State Fair's second prize for *The Harbor.*[147] Later that fall, the Paynes established themselves in Los Angeles, with a residence on Reno Street and a studio on South New Hampshire Avenue. The artist's success continued at the Stendahl Galleries. The spring exhibition, consisting of mountain and marine paintings, was the first to be accompanied by an illustrated catalogue, which included glowing essays by Payne's best supporters, Antony Anderson and Fred Hogue. Shortly thereafter, Sonia Wolfson of the *California Graphic* described Payne as a "painter of national reputation."[148]

In 1926, Payne was elected president of the California Art Club, but he soon resigned so that he could devote his full attention to painting. That summer, he returned to the Sierra, selecting the highest peaks as subjects for new work. October marked an abrupt change in direction with a move to Westport, Connecticut, where Payne hoped to expand his eastern markets. He stayed until the following spring and then left for Chicago, exhibiting there and then returning to California. This time, his family stayed behind so Evelyn could finish the school year.

Payne spent the summer of 1927 sketching in the Sierra and then received a commission to produce eight large paintings for the new Hotel St. Paul in Los Angeles. Subjects included fishing boats of France and Italy, wagons crossing the West, and the Sierra.[149] Although most reviewers continued to shower him with accolades, Arthur Millier was the first to call for change:

> Payne is unusually adroit at making a highly
> decorative picture out of somewhat worn
> material. He can combine the same kind of boats
> and sails and white-walled houses with the
> same kind of harbor water in a manner almost
> kaleidoscopic, and the result is invariably a very
> acceptable picture, colorful and well composed.
> A reviewer, of course, is always aching for
> something fresh, hot off the bat of inspiration,
> but it is well to reflect that the reviewer does
> not buy the pictures and that the public just
> as definitely longs for something like the artist
> painted last month.[150]

Payne recognized some truth in Millier's words; he too was restless and searching for inspiration. In the fall of 1927, he moved his family to Spuyten Duyvil, in the Riverdale section of the Bronx in New York City, and opened a studio on Broadway. But his continued travels proved too much. Ailing from exhaustion and pneumonia, he was confined to his apartment for several weeks, but even then he worked quietly and industriously on small gouaches.[151]

Once recovered, Payne became an active member of the New York art community, joining the Salmagundi Club and The American Artists Professional League, the latter having been established in early 1928. He was greatly sympathetic to the league's goals, which included promoting a new interest in realism, fostering cooperation among American artists, building the prestige of native art and artists, and encouraging American people to acquire American art.[152] Payne was, in fact, deeply skeptical of American patrons and audiences, especially those from California and the Southwest, where he believed the rate of "art illiteracy" to be the "highest in two continents."[153] Nevertheless, he continued to send work west from New York for exhibition. In January 1928, he held an exhibition at the Wilshire Galleries in Los Angeles with Dedrick Stuber. He also traveled to Ogden, Utah, to arrange an exhibition to be held that July. With $5,000 from the Hotel St. Paul commission, the family made another trip to Europe late that spring. After spending the summer in Chioggia and Concarneau, the family returned to New York in late September. While Payne was away, the Bartlett Galleries in Los Angeles exhibited his landscapes alongside those of San Diego artist Maurice Braun.

In December, the National Academy of Design purchased Payne's California painting *Fifth Lake [High Sierra]* (p. 92), painted near Big Pine, through the Henry Ward Ranger Fund.[154] Payne returned to California in the spring of 1929, traveling via Chicago, where he exhibited work at the Allerton Galleries, and Ogden, Utah, where he arranged for another exhibition. In Los Angeles that June, he exhibited twenty-six paintings at the Biltmore Salon in the Biltmore Hotel in Los Angeles, including scenes of the Sierra, the Swiss Alps, and Italian and French fishing boats. After the school year was over, Payne's family joined him in Laguna Beach, which now boasted a brand-new art gallery, an outgrowth of the one Payne had helped establish a decade earlier.[155] Their reunion with Laguna friends was short-lived. In early July, the Paynes set off for a sketching trip in the Canadian Rockies.

Payne returned to New York in the fall, and in the ensuing years he exhibited there, in Chicago, and in cities in Utah. He began to spend more time in the Southwest, making treks to Utah's Zion and Bryce Canyons in the summer of 1930 and then traveling to New Mexico. He spent that winter in New York, but in the summer he returned to California, where Elsie later joined him. The couple spent the next winter there, though Evelyn remained in school in New York. In the summer of 1932, the Paynes reunited in what would be their last family sketching trip to the Sierra, and then they separated. Elsie moved to an apartment in Los Angeles and Evelyn entered the University of California, Los Angeles; Edgar eventually settled in a studio-home on North Seward Street in Hollywood (p. 94). It was a tumultuous time. In 1932, Payne also parted ways with his longtime dealer Earl Stendahl.[156]

Although the Paynes were living apart, they remained in close contact. In June 1934, Payne exhibited at Elsie's new gallery, the Payne-Kann Studio Gallery in Beverly Hills, which she had opened with Marie H. Kann.[157] He also continued to exhibit at

Fifth Lake [High Sierra], c. 1928. Oil on canvas, 40⅜ x 50¼ in. Smithsonian American Art Museum, Washington, DC. Bequest of Henry Ward Ranger through the National Academy of Design, 1957.10.6. Image courtesy of the Smithsonian American Art Museum, Washington, DC / Art Resource, NY

Lake Louise, c. 1929. Oil on canvas, 28 x 34 in. Collection of Thomas T. Tatum

other venues in Los Angeles and San Francisco. At his Hollywood studio, he taught eager students the techniques and principles of landscape painting. He was highly respected by his pupils, who admired his commitment to representational art. Yet he was no longer considered avant-garde—even by California standards.

Payne felt keenly the threat posed by modernism and abstraction and remained steadfast in his commitment to landscape painting, advocating equal exhibition privileges for those artists choosing to work in a more traditional manner. He was vocal, and sometimes even radical, in his views, going so far as to publish a newspaper article insinuating that the moderns of the art world were Communists held under

the "deepest crimson" influence of "Bolshevik control."[158] On October 4, 1939, Payne met with other Southern California artists to champion traditional methods and form a Los Angeles branch of the Society for Sanity in Art. The society had been founded in Chicago in 1936 by Josephine Hancock Logan; its Los Angeles branch was one of sixteen throughout the United States. Unequivocally opposed to abstraction and other modern styles, the society aimed to encourage art "based on sound, fundamental principles," art that its members deemed "sane, understandable and built upon tradition and precedent of the past as well as new, contemporary ideas."[159] Promoting quality and craftsmanship, the organization sought to foster realism through exhibitions, lectures, and activities. Payne immediately became a charter member of the Los Angeles branch and wrote the introduction to its first exhibition catalogue in 1940. Like Payne, many of the artists who contributed to the society's displays had previously been prizewinners; many now had trouble even getting their work accepted into shows. For them, the Society for Sanity in Art became an important exhibition venue.

For Payne, active participation in the conservative society's exhibitions and activities was not enough. So sure was he of his methods and beliefs that he went one step further in bringing his convictions about landscape painting to a larger audience (opposite, pp. 96, 97). In 1941, after nine months of writing, he completed and self-published *Composition of Outdoor Painting,* "a short and concise handbook on the essentials of outdoor painting for the practical student."[160] In it, through essays and illustrations of his own paintings and those by others, he promoted traditional practices, communicating what he had learned over

Edgar Payne at His Seward Street Studio, n.d. Photographer unknown. Courtesy of DeRu's Fine Arts

"Problems in Perspective," original layout for *Composition of Outdoor Painting* by Edgar Payne
(Hollywood, CA: Seward, 1941)

"Arrangements of Picture Design, European Artists," original layout for *Composition of Outdoor Painting* by Edgar Payne (Hollywood, CA: Seward, 1941)

"Predominating Light or Dark Masses," original layout for *Composition of Outdoor Painting* by Edgar Payne (Hollywood, CA: Seward, 1941)

the course of his career and aiming to convince a new generation of painters of the legitimacy—even superiority—of representational landscape painting. The book "created a sensation" and was a popular success, making Payne an artistic celebrity of sorts and earning him an endorsement deal for Schmincke Finest, a line of artists' oil paints (below).[161]

As Payne neared the end of his life, his nomadic journey slowed, although he continued to paint and exhibit. In 1946, he was diagnosed with cancer. Elsie, who had been his caretaker when they were together,

closed her studio on Wilshire Boulevard and moved into his Hollywood home. She cared for him until his passing, on April 8, 1947. Despite Edgar's failing health, the couple's last year together was among the happiest of their lives. In the month that he died, Payne exhibited a final Sierra painting, *Temple Crags,* at the Laguna Beach Art Association.[162]

In tribute to his accomplishments, memorial exhibitions followed. The Laguna Beach Art Association held the first that August in a combined showing with Payne's friend and colleague William Wendt, who had died the previous December. In early 1948, the Bowers Museum in Santa Ana, the Hollywood and Riverside public libraries, the Hollywood Athletic Club, and the Ebell Club of Los Angeles held solo memorial exhibitions; Occidental College and Pomona College organized displays in 1949. Yet by the 1950s and 1960s, Payne exhibitions were few. His achievements went largely unrecognized until the late 1960s, when the Southeast Arkansas Arts and Science Center organized an exhibition titled *The World of Edgar Payne.* In 1970, the Kennedy Galleries in New York hosted the largest retrospective to date, assembling sixty-five of Payne's paintings and drawings. Elsie Payne lived just long enough to see this revival of interest, although she must have been disappointed with the complete lack of New York sales. She continued her own artistic production into her mid-eighties, at which time she moved to Minneapolis to live with her daughter and son-in-law.[163]

Advertisement for Schmincke Finest Artists' Oil Colors. *Art Digest,* September 1, 1941. Image courtesy of the California State Library, California History Section

It is, perhaps, understandable that Payne's reputation languished. The artistic vanguard in California and elsewhere in the 1950s had moved well beyond Payne's deeply held adherence to subject and the landscape. Now focusing solely on the formal properties of art, many forgot—or chose to ignore—just how important these same properties had been to Payne, whose art was founded on carefully constructed compositions; balanced, glowing color; and shimmering paint handling. Although in their day these paintings were described as "most modern, but modern with a keen sense of decency and the fitness of things," it was exactly this decency and fitness that were now derided.[164] Payne's own frequently voiced opinions about abstraction and other contemporary trends fueled this antagonism, making his paintings an easy target of ridicule and neglect.[165]

Yet it was only a matter of time before California artists once again turned to local light and terrain. The West's open spaces and salubrious climate had never seemed as conducive to dark, painterly abstraction as did New York's immense structures and oppressive, brooding atmosphere, and thus the Golden State's deeply rooted tradition of landscape painting became newly viable. A new generation turned to Payne's book, *Composition of Outdoor Painting,* which went into its third printing in 1957, just as this heyday of Abstract Expressionism began to wane. A respect for representation reemerged, and Southern California's light and color, and the transcendent scale of its landscape, offered new possibilities. Roadside architecture by Ed Ruscha, the swimming-pool paintings of David Hockney, the ethereal, light-filled works of Robert Irwin, and the evocative Ocean Park paintings of Richard Diebenkorn all stemmed from California's Southland.

This renewed enthusiasm ultimately helped foster a new critical appreciation for Payne's work and resulted in his 1969 and 1970 retrospectives. The fact that the largest of these exhibitions took place in New York, the center of the art world, would have pleased him, for he had never truly left a mark there. Yet, over the course of his remarkable career, he did leave behind iconic works of California, the desert Southwest, Switzerland, France, and Italy. His travels were in service of capturing something broader than could be realized in any single locale. He ultimately hoped that his work would transcend place and, by extension, broadly emblematize his time, his deep love of nature, and his passion for painting. He also fervently believed that one day he would be thought of not as a regional specialist of mountains, boats, or desert but as an American painter who left behind a rich visual record of an incredible scenic journey.

Sunset in the Foothills, n.d. Oil on canvas, 32½ x 39½ in.
Collection of D. L. Stuart Jr.

NOTES

1. Fred S. Hogue, "Edgar Alwin Payne and His Art," in *Edgar Alwin Payne and His Work,* by Antony Anderson and Fred S. Hogue (Los Angeles: Stendahl Art Galleries, 1926), 12.

2. "From Boats to Surrealism," *Los Angeles Times,* March 27, 1932.

3. Edgar A. Payne, *Composition of Outdoor Painting* (Hollywood, CA: Seward, 1941); repr., 7th ed., ed. DeRu's Fine Arts with addenda by Evelyn Payne Hatcher (Bellflower, CA: DeRu's Fine Arts, 2005), 49. Page references are to the 2005 edition.

4. Antony Anderson, "Edgar Alwin Payne: A Biography and an Appreciation," in Anderson and Hogue, *Payne and His Work,* 8.

5. Payne, *Composition of Outdoor Painting,* 26.

6. Fred Hogue, "Grandeur of California Sierras: Paints Sunset Glow and Morning Light," *Hemet (CA) News,* July 1, 1927; S. Fred Hogue, "The Art of Edgar Alwyn [sic] Payne," *Los Angeles Times,* May 23, 1926.

7. Hogue, "Grandeur of California Sierras."

8. Evelyn Payne Hatcher, "Planning Compositions," in *The Drawings of Edgar Payne, 1883–1947,* with introduction by Jean Stern (Minneapolis, MN: Payne Studios, 2002), 109.

9. It is not possible to definitively assign an exact place or date of Payne's birth. The State of Missouri—and more specifically Barry County, where the artist was born—did not officially record births or deaths until 1910. There is no question that the artist was born in Barry County, although the location has been cited as being near Washburn or near Cassville. Either assertion is essentially true, as the towns are less than nine miles apart, and the Payne farm was probably somewhere in between. Payne's younger sister, Nora, for instance, was born in Seligman, just south of Washburn. One of the most credible documents, Payne's emergency passport application dated August 27, 1924, states that he was born near Cassville.

   As to Payne's date of birth, census records and other official documents are inconsistent, even documents signed by the artist himself. The 1900 census, for instance, taken on June 4, 1900, when Payne was living with his parents in Prairie Grove, Arkansas, lists his age as seventeen and his date of birth as March 1883.

   The 1910 census, taken on April 16, when Payne was in Chicago, gives his age as twenty-eight, making his birth year 1882. The 1920 census, taken on January 2, when Payne was in Laguna Beach, California, gives Payne's age as thirty-seven, again implying an 1882 date. The 1930 census, taken on April 11, when Payne was living in the Bronx in New York City, lists his age as forty-eight, making his date of birth 1882. The artist's draft registration card, which he signed on September 7, 1918, lists March 1, 1882. His European driver's license, which he signed on August 25, 1922, lists March 1, 1883. His August 27, 1924, passport application lists March 1, 1883. Various ship passenger lists log his date and place of birth as 1883, Cassville, Missouri. The California Death Index, which contains information probably submitted by Elsie, lists March 1, 1882. A biographical card in the California State Library, Sacramento, completed by Elsie after her husband's death, lists March 1, 1882. In 2002, the artist's daughter published a book titled *The Drawings of Edgar Payne, 1883–1947.* Rena Neumann Coen, the artist's primary biographer, also uses 1883 in her book *The Paynes, Edgar & Elsie: American Artists.* I would like to thank Joyce Cusick, Barry County Genealogical & Historical Society, for her help with the census and ship records.

10. Quoted in Wanda Corn, *The Color of Mood: American Tonalism, 1880–1910* (San Francisco: M. H. de Young Memorial Museum and California Palace of the Legion of Honor, 1972), 12.

11. David C. Huntington, "The Quest for Unity: American Art Between the World's Fairs, 1876–1893," in *The Quest for Unity: American Art Between the World's Fairs, 1876–1893* (Detroit: Detroit Institute of Arts, 1983), 17.

12. Payne, *Composition of Outdoor Painting,* 21, 17.

13. George Wharton James, *California, Romantic and Beautiful* (Boston: Page Company, 1914), 394–395.

14. Laura Bride Powers, "Art and Artists Around the Bay," *Oakland Tribune,* June 1916, newspaper clipping, Archives of the Oakland Museum of California.

15. Antony Anderson, Of Art and Artists, *Los Angeles Times,* April 8, 1917.

16. Theodore Steele, "In the Far West," typescript of lecture delivered at the Portfolio Club in Indianapolis, IN, 1903, Archives of American Art, Smithsonian Institution,

Washington, DC, 10. Quoted in William H. Gerdts, "The Land of Sunshine," in *Masters of Light: Plein-Air Painting in California, 1890–1930,* by Jean Stern and William H. Gerdts (Irvine, CA: The Irvine Museum, 2002), 30–31.

17. Payne wrote, "Skill in handling pigment is in itself beautiful." Payne, *Composition of Outdoor Painting,* 17.

18. Antony Anderson, Art and Artists, *Los Angeles Times,* September 3, 1911.

19. "The Meeting of the East and the West in Art: Illustrated by Examples from the Galleries of Cannell and Chaffin," *California Southland,* February–March 1920, 16.

20. Anderson, Of Art and Artists, September 28, 1919.

21. Everett C. Maxwell, "Exhibition of California Art Club," *Fine Arts Journal* 28 (January–June 1913): 189.

22. Fred Hogue, "The God of the Mountains," *Los Angeles Times,* May 22, 1927; also Hogue, "Grandeur of California Sierras."

23. Edgar Payne, quoted in Hogue, "God of the Mountains."

24. Payne, *Composition of Outdoor Painting,* 45.

25. Payne exhibited at the Pacific Southwest Exposition. Lannie Haynes Martin, article written for Arthur Millier column Art and Artists, *Los Angeles Times,* August 5, 1928.

26. Payne, *Composition of Outdoor Painting,* 63–64.

27. Ibid., vii.

28. Hatcher, "Planning Compositions," xi.

29. Rena Neumann Coen, *The Paynes, Edgar & Elsie: American Artists* (Minneapolis, MN: Payne Studios, 1988), 51.

30. "Payne Art Pleasing and Intelligible," *Chicago Daily Tribune,* June 27, 1914.

31. Hatcher, "Planning Compositions," 109.

32. Edgar Lloyd Hampton, "Los Angeles as an American Art Centre," *Current History* 24 (September 1926): 860. Quoted in Iris H. W. Engstrand, "In Search of the Sun," in *California Light, 1900–1930,* ed. Patricia Trenton and William H. Gerdts (Laguna Beach, CA: Laguna Art Museum, 1990), 58.

33. Coen, *Paynes, Edgar & Elsie,* 9.

34. Payne Pictorials, announcement of screening of *Sierra Journey* to be held at Bell and Howell Auditorium, Los Angeles, March 1, 1946, Edgar and Elsie Palmer Payne Papers, DeRu's Fine Arts, Bellflower, CA.

35. Anderson, Of Art and Artists, February 12, 1922.

36. For a discussion of the "scenic" in art, see John Ott, "Landscapes of Consumption: Auto Tourism and Visual Culture in California, 1920–1940," in *Reading California: Art, Image, and Identity, 1900–2000,* ed. Stephanie Barron, Sheri Bernstein, and Ilene Susan Fort (Los Angeles: Los Angeles County Museum of Art; Berkeley: University of California Press, 2000), 56.

37. Payne, *Composition of Outdoor Painting,* 63.

38. I would like to thank Eric Jessen, museum environmental consultant and retired chief of the Orange County Harbors, Beaches and Parks Department. With the assistance of Gregory N. Horvath, he identified the locations of numerous Payne landscapes in remote eastern Sierra locations and compared the topography and vegetation of actual sites with Payne's canvases. He documented his research in a report to the Pasadena Museum of California Art, "Terrain Provenance of Edgar Payne Canvases in the Sierra Nevada Mountains of California," December 9, 2010. Jessen was also instrumental in identifying locations of Payne's coastal scenes as documented in "Terrain Provenance of Edgar Payne Shoreline Canvases in Laguna Beach, California," December 9, 2010.

39. H. Raymond Henry, "Painter's Work on Behalf of the Southland Art Told By Writer," newspaper clipping, Ferdinand Perrett Papers, Archives of American Art, Smithsonian Institution, Washington, DC, reel no. 3862, frame 50.

40. Helen Lukens Gaut, "Motoring in Southern California," *Craftsman* 22 (August 1912): 515.

41. Ibid.

42. "At the Turn of the Wheel," *Standard Oil Bulletin* 9 (June 1921): 3. Quoted in Ott, "Landscapes of Consumption," 56.

43. Frederick Roland Miner, "California: The Landscapist's Land of Heart's Desire," *Western Art* 1 (June–August 1914): 31.

44. Evelyn Payne Hatcher, "California Mountains (the Sierra Nevada)," in *Drawings of Edgar Payne,* 53.

45. Antony Anderson, "Edgar Payne, Painter and World Traveler," *Laguna Beach South Coast News,* June 21, 1929; Coen, *Paynes, Edgar & Elsie,* 51.

46. Coen, *Paynes, Edgar & Elsie,* 25–26; Edwin Markham, *California the Wonderful: Her Romantic History, Her Picturesque People, Her Wild Shores, Her Desert Mystery, Her Valley Loveliness, Her Mountain Glory, Including Her Varied Resources, Her Commercial Greatness, Her Intellectual Achievements, Her Expanding Hopes, with Glimpses of Oregon and Washington, Her Northern Neighbors* (New York: Hearst's International Library, 1914), 267.

47. Elsie Palmer Payne, "Edgar Payne: Biographical Notes," undated, unpublished typescript, Edgar and Elsie Palmer Payne Papers, DeRu's Fine Arts, Bellflower, CA, 8.

48. Hatcher, *Drawings of Edgar Payne,* xi.

49. Miner, "California," 31.

50. Markham, *California the Wonderful,* 250.

51. Hogue, "God of the Mountains."

52. Anderson and Hogue, *Payne and His Work,* 31.

53. Agnes Elding Pallen, "Artist Celebrities Find Ideal Homes in California: Famous Painters of World Get Inspiration for Work amid Southland's Romance," *Los Angeles Times,* January 17, 1926.

54. Hogue, "Grandeur of California Sierras."

55. Caroline Walker, "Art Exhibition Vivifies Cal. Mountains," newspaper clipping, 1926, Edgar and Elsie Palmer Payne Papers, DeRu's Fine Arts, Bellflower, CA.

56. Hatcher, "California Mountains," 53.

57. Evelyn Payne Hatcher, quoted in "Payne: Biographical Notes," 7.

58. Markham, *California the Wonderful,* 264.

59. John Elder, introduction to *Nature/Walking,* by Ralph Waldo Emerson and Henry David Thoreau (Boston: Beacon Press, 1991), xvi.

60. Hogue, "God of the Mountains."

61. Frank Norris, quoted in David Wyatt, *The Fall into Eden: Landscape and Imagination in California* (Cambridge: Cambridge University Press, 1986; repr. 1988), 105–106. Page reference is to the 1988 edition.

62. Henry David Thoreau, "Walden," in *Great Short Works of Henry David Thoreau,* ed. Wendell Glick (New York: HarperPerennial, 1993), 237; Payne, *Composition of Outdoor Painting,* 45.

63. Payne, *Composition of Outdoor Painting,* 32.

64. Hatcher, *Drawings of Edgar Payne,* xi.

65. Emerson and Thoreau, *Nature/Walking,* 59.

66. Payne, *Composition of Outdoor Painting,* 44, viii.

67. The Payne children, in order of birth, were Fleda, Edgar Alwin, Nora, Robert Thomas, George William, Hereford Lamar, Alonzo, and John Burl.

68. In the 1900 census, John H. Payne's occupation is listed as "carpenter" and Edgar's is listed as "carpenter apprentice." "Schedule No. 1.—Population," *Twelfth Census of the United States,* June 4, 1900.

69. Coen, *Paynes, Edgar & Elsie,* 3–4.

70. Anderson, Of Art and Artists, February 20, 1921.

71. "California on Canvas," *San Diego Sun,* April 6, 1921.

72. Gordon St. Clair, quoted in Coen, *Paynes, Edgar & Elsie,* 8. Newspaper clippings of Gordon St. Clair's articles "Edgar Payne Is Tremendous Worker at Chosen Vocation" and "The Edgar Payne Exhibition" are included in the Edgar and Elsie Palmer Payne Papers, DeRu's Fine Arts, Bellflower, CA.

73. Anderson, Art and Artists, September 17, 1911.

74. Coen, *Paynes, Edgar & Elsie,* 9.

75. Anderson, Art and Artists, September 3, 1911.

76. Coen, *Paynes, Edgar & Elsie,* 11.

77. *Chicago Evening Post,* May 10, 1913.

78. Anderson, Of Art and Artists, February 20, 1921.

79. "Payne Art Pleasing," *Chicago Daily Tribune.*

80. A typescript chronology in the Edgar and Elsie Palmer Payne Papers, DeRu's Fine Arts, Bellflower, CA, includes the following statement: "Took enough pirate pictures to illustrate all of RLS and put production of Howard Pyle to shame."

81. Coen, *Paynes, Edgar & Elsie,* 18.

82. Albrecht Montgelas, "Payne Shows Realism on Canvas," newspaper clipping, 1916, Edgar and Elsie Palmer Payne Papers, DeRu's Fine Arts, Bellflower, CA.

83. Powers, "Around the Bay."

84. Edgar Alwin Payne, "World Peace," undated, unpublished typescript, Edgar and Elsie Palmer Payne Papers, DeRu's Fine Arts, Bellflower, CA.

85. Payne, *Composition of Outdoor Painting*, 27.

86. In 1912, Ritschel produced a painting of Monterey cypresses titled *The Fallen Comrade*. Others also produced landscapes and seascapes meant to metaphorically represent war. Armin Hansen created a symbolic painting, *War*, and William Posey Silva produced a seascape, *Peace and War*, which included the ghostly outline of a battleship on the horizon.

87. Payne, *Composition of Outdoor Painting*, 28.

88. Anderson, Art and Artists, August 19, 1906.

89. Payne, *Composition of Outdoor Painting*, 10.

90. Ibid., 7.

91. Payne was referring to a work by Frederick J. Waugh. Ibid., 57.

92. Antony Anderson, In the Realm of Art, *Los Angeles Times*, March 9, 1919.

93. Anderson, Of Art and Artists, February 12, 1922.

94. Anderson, Of Art and Artists, February 20, 1921.

95. Payne, *Composition of Outdoor Painting*, 96.

96. Markham, *California the Wonderful*, 251.

97. Ibid., 255.

98. Robert Louis Stevenson, quoted ibid., 252.

99. Robinson Jeffers, "Tamar," in *Roan Stallion, Tamar, and Other Poems* (New York: Peter G. Boyle, 1924; repr., New York: Boni & Liveright, 1925), 108. Page references are to the 1925 edition.

100. Jeffers, "Continent's End," in *Roan Stallion*, 252.

101. In 1919, Anna Cora Winchell noted in the *San Francisco Chronicle* that Payne had submitted two panel pictures to the Schussler Galleries that showed "decorative, though delicate handling." "The landscape of mountain ranges and intervening valleys is treated in pastel tints and offers the temptation to be ornate," she reported, "but the simplicity of Payne's style has given the pictures a more desirable note." Anna Cora Winchell, Artists and Their Work, *San Francisco Chronicle*, April 27, 1919. She also noted Payne's "delicate tints of pastel" in an exhibition later that year. Winchell, Artists and Their Work, September 21, 1919.

102. Hatcher, "California Mountains," 53.

103. "Twelve Masters at Pasadena," *Los Angeles Times*, August 26, 1928.

104. Hogue, "God of the Mountains." According to Eric Jessen, Payne Lake is located on the north side of the Glacier Divide, approximately 2.2 miles northwest of Goethe Peak and 0.3 mile southeast of Packsaddle Lake. Payne Lake drains into Packsaddle Lake, which drains into Piute Creek west of Piute Pass. Jessen, "Terrain Provenance," 7.

105. Michael Williams, "A Pageant of American Art," *Art and Progress* 6 (August 1915): 353.

106. Theodore Roosevelt, "Nationalism in Literature and Art," in *The Works of Theodore Roosevelt*, national ed., vol. 12 (New York: Scribner's Sons, 1926), 336.

107. Anderson, Of Art and Artists, April 22, 1923.

108. James Bryce, *The American Commonwealth*, vol. 2 (New York: Macmillan, 1912), 892.

109. Robert Henri, quoted in *The Modern West: American Landscapes, 1890–1950,* by Emily Ballew Neff and Barry Lopez (New Haven, CT: Yale University Press; Houston, TX: Museum of Fine Arts, Houston, 2006), 120.

110. *Peoria Journal*, newspaper clipping, 1917, Edgar and Elsie Palmer Payne Papers, DeRu's Fine Arts, Bellflower, CA.

111. Markham, *California the Wonderful*, 266.

112. Millier, Art and Artists, May 22, 1927.

113. Anderson, Of Art and Artists, February 12, 1922.

114. Hogue, "Grandeur of California Sierras."

115. Sonia Wolfson, "Art and Artists: Payne and Gilbert at Stendahl's," *California Graphic*, May 28, 1927.

116. "At Newcomb & Macklin's," "Magazine of the Art World," supplement, *Chicago Evening Post*, April 7, 1925.

117. Edgar Payne, quoted in Hogue, "God of the Mountains."

118. Frank Norris, "The Frontier Gone at Last," *World's Work* 3 (1902): 1728–1731. Reprinted in *The Call of the Wild: 1900–1916,* ed. Roderick Nash (New York: George Braziller, 1970), 69–71.

119. Hogue, "Art of Edgar Payne."

120. Richard Longstreth, *On the Edge of the World: Four Architects in San Francisco at the Turn of the Century* (New York: Architectural History Foundation; Cambridge, MA: MIT Press, 1983), 111.

121. George Wharton James, "J. Bond Francisco: Musician and Painter," *Out West* 6 (September 1913): 92. Quoted in Jasper G. Schad, "'A City of Picture Buyers': Art, Identity, and Aspiration in Los Angeles and Southern California, 1891–1914," *Southern California Quarterly* 92 (Spring 2010): 31.

122. Markham, *California the Wonderful,* 267.

123. Mary Austin, "The Land of Little Rain," in *The Literature of California: Writings from the Golden State,* vol. 1, ed. Jack Hicks et al. (Berkeley: University of California Press, 2000), 388.

124. Coen, *Paynes, Edgar & Elsie,* 23.

125. Sir John Gilbert, quoted in Payne, *Composition of Outdoor Painting,* 2.

126. Members of The Trailers included Irwin St. John Tucker (founder and secretary), Victor Higgins (president), Edgar Payne (first vice president), and Charles Francis Browne (second vice president), along with Gustave Baumann, E. Martin Hennings, Frank Peyraud, Samuel Kennedy, Ethel Coe, Leila Marshall, Ralph Fletcher Seymour, Enoch and Edna Vognild, O. Irwin Myers, Willard Best, Nell Devine, Florence Hall, and Dorothy Tucker. I would like to thank Ellen Halteman, Director of Collections, California State Parks, for her help in identifying the railroad.

127. Evelyn Payne Hatcher, "Arizona and New Mexico," in *Drawings of Edgar Payne,* 79.

128. Conrad Buff, cited in Coen, *Paynes, Edgar & Elsie,* 21. Reports of the true scale of the project vary widely. Critic Antony Anderson wrote of Payne's 26,000 square yards of canvas and 67,000 pounds of white lead paint. Anderson, "Payne: A Biography," 9.

129. Coen, *Paynes, Edgar & Elsie,* 21.

130. Elsie Payne, quoted ibid., 23.

131. Evelyn Payne Hatcher, "Versatility," in *Drawings of Edgar Payne,* 65–67.

132. Anna A. Hills, "The Laguna Beach Art Association," *American Magazine of Art* 10 (October 1919): 463.

133. Ibid.

134. "The New Art Gallery in Laguna," *Critique* 1 (Spring 1929): 21.

135. Anderson, Of Art and Artists, August 10, 1919.

136. Anderson, Of Art and Artists, January 30, 1921. In 1922 Alma May Cook called him one of California's "best painters." Alma May Cook, "Edgar Payne to Tour in Europe," *Los Angeles Express,* May 22, 1922.

137. Jessen, "Terrain Provenance," 4–6.

138. Anderson, Of Art and Artists, February 12, 1922.

139. Ibid., May 28, 1922.

140. "Tribute Paid Noted Artist," *Los Angeles Times,* May 23, 1922.

141. Anderson, Of Art and Artists, April 22, 1923.

142. Edgar Payne, letter from Switzerland, April 15, 1923. Quoted in "Payne: Biographical Notes," 8.

143. "At Newcomb & Macklin's," *Chicago Evening Post.*

144. Edgar Payne, quoted in Anderson, Of Art and Artists, November 12, 1922.

145. [Antony Anderson], "Some Newsy Notes on Matters of Art," *Los Angeles Times,* May 31, 1925.

146. Hogue, "Payne and His Art," 15.

147. Coen, *Paynes, Edgar & Elsie,* 50.

148. Wolfson, "Payne and Gilbert at Stendahl's."

149. "Studies in the Decorative," *Los Angeles Times,* August 7, 1927.

150. Millier, Art and Artists, May 22, 1927.

151. Coen, *Paynes, Edgar & Elsie,* 53, 95.

152. Neeta Marquis, "Artist Back After Absence: Pictures Placed on Exhibition," *Los Angeles Times,* June 23, 1929.

153. "Gossip from Studios," *Los Angeles Times,* August 19, 1928.

154. According to Eric Jessen, this canvas depicts scenery up the south fork of Big Pine Canyon, including North Palisade and Polemonium Peak. Fifth Lake itself was imported into the scene from the north fork of Big Pine

Creek, a distance of approximately 2.4 miles to the northwest. Jessen, "Terrain Provenance," 3.

155. Payne contributed to the Laguna Beach Art Association's 1927 *Building Fund Exhibition,* which was held to raise money for construction of the association's new gallery. He also exhibited in its 1929 opening show.

156. Stendahl was hurt but also relieved. He wrote to artist Jessie Botke, "As far as Payne is concerned, it looks like a personal feeling against me. Had Payne come to me and stated what he wanted to do [switch galleries], I possibly would have helped him all I could. This is going to be more or less of a relief to me as I have carried a personal responsibility on my shoulders where the artist depended on most of his income thru me." Letter from Earl Stendahl, 3006 Wilshire Boulevard, Los Angeles, to Jessie Botke, Wheeler Canyon, Santa Paula, CA, May 25, 1932, Stendahl Art Gallery Records, Archives of American Art, Smithsonian Institution, Washington, DC.

157. A few months later the gallery became the Payne-Pegler Studio Gallery, when Virginia Pegler replaced Marie Kann. Elsie opened the Elsie Palmer Payne Art School and Gallery in September 1936, after her partnership with Pegler ended.

158. Edgar Payne, "Bolshevik Control Seen in 'New' Art: Noted Artist Flays 'Red' Influence in Expression," newspaper clipping, Edgar and Elsie Palmer Payne Papers, DeRu's Fine Arts, Bellflower, CA. Also in Payne's papers is an article by Glare Sheridan, "The Philosophy of Art," *International Studio,* April 1924, which bears a typed inscription: "To refute claims that *no* Communist influence exists in so-called modern art, two pages from the April 1924 issue of the International Studio (The 'Bible' of the Art World of that period) [are] here reproduced."

159. Coen, *Paynes, Edgar & Elsie,* 74.

160. Payne, *Composition of Outdoor Painting,* vi.

161. "Edgar A. Payne, Noted Painter, Writer, Uses Schmincke Finest Artists' Oil Colors," advertisement, *Art Digest,* September 1, 1941.

162. Coen, *Paynes, Edgar & Elsie,* 80.

163. She died there on June 17, 1971.

164. "Edgar A. Payne Opens One-Man Show on 15th at Stendahl Gallery," *Laguna Beach Life,* May 14, 1926.

165. Payne told Antony Anderson, "I have not seen any modern painting that has any 'punch' to it, and think it is a great deal like what Mark Twain said about the report of his death—that it is 'greatly exaggerated.'" Anderson, Of Art and Artists, November 12, 1922.

"All the Paintable Things in Europe"

PAYNE'S EUROPEAN ART AND TRAVELS (1922–1924, 1928)

Lisa N. Peters, PhD

Director of Research and Publications
Spanierman Gallery

Throughout his career, Edgar Payne demonstrated indomitable persistence. Only a few years after he visited the High Sierra for the first time, in 1917–1918, he had become the Sierra's leading interpreter, enduring blistering conditions and trekking into remote stretches that other artists did not attempt. "His chafed feet are bleeding and his brain reels, but he perseveres for he is a true artist," an article noted in 1921.[1] Payne showed a similar intrepid determination in his plans for a trip to Europe. At the time of Payne's departure, in the summer of 1922, the *Los Angeles Times* art critic Antony Anderson (writing under the pseudonym of Vandyke Brown) reported that in two years the artist expected "to paint all the paintable things in Europe." Anderson was certain that Payne could fulfill such an ambitious aim, stating, "If anybody can cover the ground in that period, Edgar can."[2] Only one year after Payne's departure with his wife, Elsie, and their daughter, Evelyn (then age eight), Anderson pronounced that Payne had in fact already met his goal, remarking that the artist had "left Los Angeles after conquering the High Sierras in paint, with the avowed purpose of vanquishing the Maritime Alps with the same medium. His exhibition proves that he has apparently done it off the bat."[3]

Over the course of his trip, which lasted until the end of the summer of 1924, Payne received accolades from the press in Los Angeles and Chicago as well as in Paris and Rome, confirming the success of his efforts. At the same time, his odyssey influenced his art more than he might have expected. Responding to the French and Swiss Alps and the fishing craft and cargo boats of the Adriatic Sea and Brittany, he united his visual impressions with abstract form, expressing the essence of his subjects while also finding in them the means to convey his reverence for nature and to refine the ideas about visual harmony that he would codify in his book of advice to artists, *Composition of Outdoor Painting* (1941).[4] Europe provided a means for Payne to solidify and enhance his artistic identity, while in painting the Alps he established a point of comparison by which to affirm the aesthetic value of the more pristine Sierra Nevada.

In terms of Payne's career, the time he spent in Europe was brief. Nonetheless, the work he produced as a result of his first trip and a second stay in France and Italy in the summer of 1928 has remained significant. Indeed, when his obituary appeared in the *New York Times*, its subheading read "Edgar Alwin Payne: Artist Was Known for Paintings of Alps and Sierras."[5] Such sequencing of Payne's subjects (repeated in the short article) indicates that his reputation in the end rested on his images of both Europe and California.

P. 108: *Brittany Boats* (detail, p. 158), c. 1924

Opposite: *Alpine Village—Switzerland*, c. 1922. Oil on canvas, 42 x 42 in. Weinstein Family Trust

FROM LOS ANGELES TO ROME
(JUNE–NOVEMBER 1922)

The *Los Angeles Times* art critic Fred Hogue wrote in 1927 that "in his youth Payne was attracted to the legend of the European Alps, and made the traditional pilgrimage to Interlocken [*sic*]."[6] However, such a pilgrimage would not take place for Payne until he was an adult, and if he had aspirations to see the Alps when he was young, he did not find a way to realize them. While Payne was in Chicago in 1913, his thoughts may have been of Paris when he was invited on the basis of his work to become a member of the Union internationale des beaux-arts et des lettres, an association of Parisian artists.[7] However, in the period that followed,

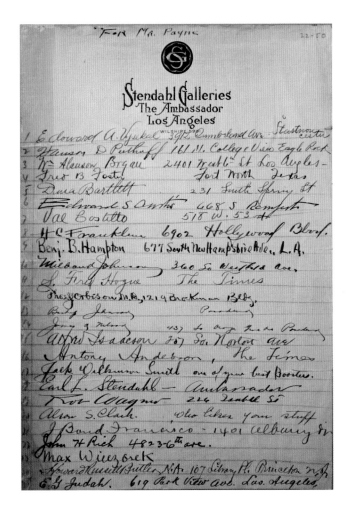

"For Mr. Payne," signatures of guests at banquet hosted by the Stendahl Galleries, May 22, 1922. Courtesy of DeRu's Fine Arts

instead of crossing the Atlantic Ocean he went west, to California and to the American Southwest. His filled itinerary left him little time for a trip to Europe, and travel restrictions during World War I no doubt also kept him homebound.

Thus, unlike many American artists who ventured to Europe early in their careers, Payne did not make the journey until he was thirty-nine years old and well established. Yet leaving at this point made sense for him: his motive was not to refine his skills through European study but to use his already well-honed artistic sensibilities to paint what he felt to be the best of European scenery. While the art community of Los Angeles speculated as to what Payne would derive from his travels abroad, at the same time urging him to return afterward to "his land of choice," many cheered him on his way at a banquet held in his honor by the Stendahl Galleries at the Ambassador Hotel on Monday, May 22, 1922, shortly before he set off.[8] Anderson reported that Earl Stendahl "tendered" the banquet and "smoker" and that "everybody was there—immortals to the traditional number of forty." He went on to note, "Most of these were artists, of course, but there were picture dealers, critics, museum directors, physicians, motion-picture directors and writers, picture lovers pure and simple, and at least one bishop."[9] Of the "immortals"—all men, all of them wearing tuxedos for the affair—twenty-five signed a sheet of Stendahl Galleries stationery headed "For Mr. Payne" (left), including Los Angeles artists Dana Bartlett, Alson Skinner Clark, John Bond Francisco, Hanson Puthuff, and Jack Wilkinson Smith.[10] The *Los Angeles Times* was represented by Anderson and Hogue, the latter delivering to the guests a radiophone address titled "California the

Beautiful." Payne had painted miniature landscapes and framed them in gold, and these were given to the guests as party favors (p. 86).

After leaving Los Angeles, the Paynes stopped in Chicago, where their departure overseas was delayed when Evelyn came down with whooping cough. This time was well used by Payne, who exhibited work at the studio of his friend Grace Hickox from July 2 through July 10.[11] At the end of July the family reached Paris, where they remained for approximately two months, residing at the Hôtel d'Athènes, near the Gare Saint-Lazare.[12] While in Paris the family made excursions, including a visit to the battlefields of the recent war.[13] Their mode of transport was a flivver, a Model T Ford that Payne would push beyond its usual limits as the family made its way through the French Alps, to Rome, and north again to Paris and Brittany (p. 115). In early November, Payne sent a

long letter to Anderson from the Riviera town of Menton in which he reported on his travels to date. In it he conveyed his impressions of Paris, noting that he found the city's museums and galleries "very interesting" but that he did not care much for the city and that modern art did not have much "punch" to it. He wrote to Anderson of his plan to live up to his "primes" for his friends in America by simply keeping busy and producing in his own manner, stating, "So far I have seen nothing in the way of painting or otherwise that would induce me to imitate any ism or creed and since coming over here I have much more respect for my own work and nationality."[14]

Leaving Paris in September, the family headed south to the French Alps, where they probably found lodgings in the town of Chamonix, situated below the looming form of the Mont Blanc massif.[15] In the period ahead, Payne explored the dramatic

Edgar Payne's Banquet Dinner Hosted by Stendahl, May 22, 1922. Photographer unknown. Courtesy of DeRu's Fine Arts

Peak at Argentière, c. 1922. Oil on canvas, 29 x 29 in. Courtesy of George Stern Fine Arts

countryside around him, which he described to Anderson as "very different from our own California mountains, but paintable and picturesque."[16] The scope of his subjects at this time may be determined by the titles of works included in the exhibition *Edgar Alwyn [sic] Payne: Recently Completed Paintings from France, Switzerland, and Italy,* which opened in April 1923 at the Stendahl Galleries. Among the paintings on view were scenes of the French Alps, including images of Mont Blanc, the highest peak in France as well as in western Europe; Saint-Gervais-les-Bains; the valley of Les Contamines; and mountain slopes, villages, and glaciers in the Haute-Savoie. At this time he also painted *Peak at Argentière* (opposite), which depicts the Argentière Glacier rising above the town of Argentière. As in scenes of the Sierra Nevada and the American Southwest, he stressed the grandeur of nature through the enormity of the mountains within the space of a picture. However, the settlements in France's high country, not present in the Sierra, challenged him in new ways, and he focused on the subtle aesthetic accommodations of man to the natural environment. In *Peak at Argentière* the red-orange roofs of valley homes echo the tones of the rocky buttes above, while a mountain glacier curves between the summit and the foothills. Five paintings of Switzerland were also included in the show, including *Alpine Vista—Switzerland* (University of Wyoming), which is strikingly similar in tone and composition to Payne's earlier Sierra scene *Rugged Slopes and Tamarack* (p. 80) but is more intimate in its perspective, and *Alpine Village—Switzerland* (pp. 110–111), in which the houses—toylike within the grand scheme—bask in the sunlight, with the cliffs rising protectively directly overhead. The diagonal of a hill in the middle ground

serves to flatten the composition as in a Japanese print, drawing together foreground and background. Payne had used square canvases in Sierra views such as *Solitude's Enchantment* (p. 84), but he turned to this format more consistently in these Alpine scenes. With such an emphasis on a dense grouping of forms oriented to the surface, Payne expressed his feeling that the Alps were more decorative than the wilder Sierra.

A peak that Payne felt driven to "vanquish," Mont Blanc, figured as his subject in two of the most important paintings to result from his trip, *Le Grand Pic Blanc,* exhibited at the Paris Salon of 1923 (p. 116), and the larger *The Great White Peak [Mt. Blanc, France]* (p. 145), which he would create in his Paris studio in 1924. In most of his known Mont Blanc scenes, his view was not, however, of the mountain's summit—a rounded hump not much higher than the other peaks rising from the Mont Blanc massif. Instead, his vantage point looked toward the Aiguille de Bionnassay, the 13,295-foot needle-like peak that is the last rise on

Edgar and the Flivver in Rome, n.d. Photographer unknown. Courtesy of DeRu's Fine Arts

Le Grand Pic Blanc, 1922. Oil on canvas, 43 x 43 in. The Ruth Stoever-Fleming Collection of Southern California Art

the shoulder of the western ridge of the Mont Blanc massif (below right).[17] This perspective of the mountain would have been visible from a stop on the Mont Blanc Tramway.[18] Payne's angle is from Bellevue, just above the torrent at Bionnassay, at an elevation of approximately 5,910 feet. That Payne hiked to a high elevation on Mont Blanc is suggested in *Slopes of Mt. Blanc* (p. 118), represented in his Stendahl Galleries exhibition, in which his viewpoint is just below the last pitch to the top of the peak. Here he included one of the shelter huts situated just below the snow line; he would later remark on the prevalence of such huts throughout the Alps.[19] In *Le Grand Pic Blanc*, Payne constructed his composition carefully, omitting the walls of the massif and a second needle-like peak just below that of the Aiguille de Bionnassay. Treating the mountain as a symmetrical shape balanced firmly within the square format of his canvas, he expressed its strength and stability. In limiting the scene's recession, he draws our gaze upward, conveying the peak's nobility as its summit, the highest point in the picture, is lightly encircled by wispy clouds. The palette, neither too bright nor too subdued, reveals a glow that seems to emanate from within the perennially white mountain, expressing its spiritual presence. Bringing together his visual impression with abstract considerations, Payne conveyed his veneration for this "monarch among monarchs," as Mont Blanc was described in poetic tributes.[20]

The Paynes left the Alps at some point in October, traveling south through Marseilles and along the Riviera to Menton, on the French-Italian border. "All along it was a dream," Payne wrote to Anderson, stating that he found Nice, Cannes, and Monaco "all beautiful" and Menton, Antibes, and Juan-les-Pins "also

picturesque." Payne observed that the Mediterranean Sea seemed bluer than the Pacific Ocean, though he qualified this remark, adding, "At least the red-tiled roofs make it appear so." Commenting that the people showed "wonderful taste in their houses," he stated, "Very seldom is a white house seen—they are all painted a warm tone, yellow or orange, and you can imagine them against a blue-green sea."[21] In *Along the Riviera, Menton, France* (p. 119), he followed guidelines he would later recommend in *Composition of Outdoor Painting,* creating an arrangement winnowed by a singular opening, consisting here of the break between the verticals of the olive trees that fan across the foreground. Through this narrowing of the space, the viewer's eye is encouraged to travel upward along the circular stair step of red roofs that climaxes in Menton's Italian Baroque Basilica of San Michel, behind which the buildings follow the descending line of the distant hills. Opposing the strong lines of the trees with the softer contours of the coastal village

Aiguille de Bionnassay, Mont Blanc, France, n.d.
Photographer unknown. Courtesy of On Foot Holidays

Slopes of Mt. Blanc, 1922–1923. Oil on canvas, 29 x 29 in. Courtesy of Redfern Gallery

Along the Riviera, Menton, France, 1922. Oil on canvas, 29 x 29 in. Collection of James Taylor and Gary Conway

nestled in the hills, Payne conveyed the harmonious and ordered nature of this lush, settled landscape. In another painting, he depicted the basilica from the water (opposite).

Payne then crossed the border into Italy, where he found artistic subjects in Rapallo and Santa Margherita on the Ligurian coast, as the titles of several works in his 1923 Stendahl Galleries exhibition indicate. In a number of these images he depicted fishing boats, representing his first exploration of a subject that became increasingly important in the period ahead.

ROME, CHIOGGIA, AND BACK TO THE ALPS (NOVEMBER 1922–SEPTEMBER 1923)

The Paynes spent the next phase of their trip in Rome, where they stayed from November 1922 until March 24, 1923. Residing in a large apartment and studio on the Piazza Dante that had housed the Belgian Academy during the war, the family endured a colder winter than expected, while Payne worked steadily to turn the pencil and oil sketches captured on his travels into larger works.[22] Whether or not the recent political events, in which Benito Mussolini staged a coup d'état supported by the Italian government, affected Edgar and Elsie Payne cannot be ascertained. After leaving Rome, the Paynes headed north to Switzerland. Reporting on this phase of the trip, Payne described visiting Tivoli, Perugia, Florence, and Genoa. Of the Palazzo Pitti and the Uffizi Gallery in Florence, he wrote in an April 15 letter that he had come away "with a most profound respect and admiration for some of the paintings; for in spite of the religious subjects some of these men could *paint.*" By contrast, he found the paintings he had seen "elsewhere in Europe" to be "more or less mediocre." Of

these, he considered only about 15 or 20 percent to be "real works of art."[23]

The family then ventured past Lake Maggiore and on to Domodossola, in Piedmont, Italy. From there they crossed into Switzerland, heading north to the Simplon Pass. Told by Italian officials that the passes into Switzerland were closed, Payne remained undeterred. Returning to Domodossola, the Paynes loaded their flivver on the train, passed through the Simplon Tunnel, and disembarked in the town of Brig, Switzerland.[24] There Payne wrote that he "took a stroll to look at the mountains and other scenery, mostly mountains. Mountains in front, rear and both sides, and reaching far up into the heavens until hidden by the clouds." Awed by his surroundings, he waxed lyrical: "To me there is no appeal like the mountains, and up here among these peaks it is almost unspeakably sublime, and I fear I shall want to spend all my time in Europe here. The interesting peaks are within a radius of fifty miles, which makes it very convenient. I find the Swiss very efficient in everything, and particularly so in the arrangement of the mountains."[25] Payne would return to this cornucopia of mountains, but in this instance the family did not stay long. Finding it too cold for Payne to sketch outdoors, they drove along the Rhône River to Lake Geneva in search of warmer weather.[26] When this did not eventuate, they changed course and headed to Venice.[27]

For countless American artists of the late nineteenth and the twentieth centuries, no tour of Europe was complete without a trip to this city. The roseate tones of marble palaces and churches against the glittering water of the Venetian Lagoon, and the picturesque gondolas gliding back and forth, had inspired artists for hundreds of years. However, Payne's only

Opposite: *Wine Boats, Menton,* c. 1923. Oil on canvas, 20 x 16 in. The James Irvine Swinden Family Collection

Santa Maria della Salute, c. 1923. Oil on board, 8 x 9 in. Helene Halperin Collection

known view of Venice itself is a small oil looking across the Grand Canal toward the Church of Santa Maria della Salute (opposite). Despite a warm reception by American artists residing in the city, the Paynes did not linger long.[28] Shortly after their arrival, they left for the island of Chioggia, located on the southern part of the Lagoon. Connected to the mainland by causeways and to the sea by an inlet of its port, the Adriatic fishing and boat-building town was the salt-producing capital of the coast and the channel by which Venice received wheat and grain from the rich farmlands of Romagna and the Marches and exported its goods to the south.[29]

Evelyn later wrote that her father chose Chioggia because of his interest in the "traditional boats with a history that goes back thousands of years."[30] Constructed in the same way since ancient times, with flat, wide hulls, huge weathered and painted sails, and curved prows, the boats conjured a timeless world. Hogue observed that Payne found in them "the fleets of Nineveh, Tyre, and of the Palestine of King Solomon" and that he was drawn to this subject because progress had bypassed "these lowly sailor folk and their craft," the latter built just as their ancestors had constructed them more than two thousand years ago.[31] That the boats were perfectly adapted to the shallow waters and light winds of the Lagoon ensured their continued use. In works such as *Marco Polo Relic, Adriatic (Thus Did We Sail for the Doge) [Italy]* (p. 125), Payne captured how these elegant forms still met the needs of fishermen, seen working below the gently billowing sails. Sharply delineating the contours of the sails against the dark waters of the Lagoon, Payne expressed the strength and permanence of these vessels, conveying their resilience through the ages.

Payne's many drawings of the boats of Chioggia included detailed views of sails and rigging as well as generalized images considering their compositional possibilities (p. 124). He also photographed the boats, taking composed pictures rather than snapshots, such as one in which a single vessel seen broadly establishes the structure of the image (p. 124). In another photograph (p. 124), Payne showed the gigantic sails of lateen-rigged boats from below against open skies, his broad horizontal format conveying the stillness and quietude of this timeless locale and the grand scale of the ancient boats that were a perpetual presence on the Lagoon. (See the essay in this catalogue by Jean Stern for further discussion of Payne's work as a photographer.) In paintings as well, he recorded the boats' features and movement while organizing them into artistic arrangements expressive of their character. In *Adriatic Cargo Boats, Chioggia, Italy* (p. 128), the vessel with unfurled sails coming toward the viewer is a *trabaccoló,* a high-prowed, wide-hulled transport boat. The signature sculpted and painted eyes adorning the front of the boat hark back to ancient Egypt, when this symbol signified powers of healing and eternal renewal.[32] In this painting and others of this period, Payne painted his backgrounds with decorative swatches of color, forgoing specific evidence of sky and clouds. Such an approach suggests a desire for his paintings to be seen as works of art rather than as scenic views belonging simply to a travelogue.

In *Venetian Boats* (p. 127), Payne portrayed *bragozzi,* two-masted fishing vessels noted for their lateen rigging. In this sort of rigging, a vessel's sails are attached to a boom that crosses the mast. The sails are adjusted by changing the boom's angle or by raising or lowering it, and Payne captured the almost

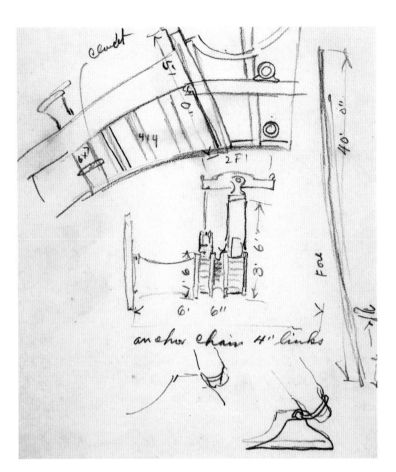

Clockwise from top left:

Details of Lateen Rigging on Adriatic Boat, n.d.
Pencil on paper, 10 x 8 in. Courtesy of DeRu's
Fine Arts

Italian Cargo Boat, Chioggia, Italy, n.d. Photograph
by Edgar Payne. Courtesy of DeRu's Fine Arts

Chioggia Boats, n.d. Photograph by Edgar Payne.
Courtesy of DeRu's Fine Arts

Marco Polo Relic, Adriatic (Thus Did We Sail for the Doge) [Italy], 1923–1924. Oil on canvas, 42 x 42 in. Collection of Ruth and Robert Mirvis

perpendicular angle at which such sails could be set. This painting reveals the way that Payne broadened his art in his focus on boats. As he explained in *Composition of Outdoor Painting*, boats, given their movement and variety of forms, pose a different set of problems from those of landscapes or buildings. Subtly organizing the boats in this work, he created an access point in the far sailboat on the left, which draws the viewer to one closer to the central grouping on the right, establishing a place of rest, while the diagonals of the vessels in the foreground convey a sense of forward motion. The result makes the viewer a participant in the animation of the scene. Indeed, Payne came to feel so strongly that boats posed

unique issues for the artist that he would propose they be given a category of their own, separate from marine views, with which they are usually grouped.[33]

The distinctive markings painted on the sails of Adriatic vessels also drew Payne's interest. Elizabeth Pennell stated in 1890 that such sails did not belong to an "everyday life of toil and struggling" but rather to "a great festival like that which graced the Lagoon on old Ascension morn."[34] In *Cargo Boats, Chioggia, Italy* (p. 129), Payne created a collage-like effect, bringing together the vibrant patterns of the boats with their painted hulls, their decorative rudders, and especially their sails, which were paintings in their own right.

Chioggia Boats at Home [Italy], n.d. Pencil on paper, 10 x 12 in. Collection of Ruth and Robert Mirvis

Venetian Boats, c. 1923. Oil on canvas, 20 x 24 in. Collection of Mr. and Mrs. Thomas B. Stiles II

Adriatic Cargo Boats, Chioggia, Italy, c. 1923. Oil on canvas, 42½ x 42½ in. Collection of D. L. Stuart Jr.

Cargo Boats, Chioggia, Italy, 1923. Oil on canvas, 43 x 43 in. The Buck Collection, Laguna Beach, California

Matterhorn, Late Afternoon, c. 1923. Oil on canvas, 53 x 53 in. Collection of Harry Parashis

The Paynes left Chioggia that summer, returning by train to Switzerland, where they stayed at the Hotel Krebs Interlaken.[35] In the heart of the Swiss Alps, the town of Interlaken provided access in all directions to magnificent mountain scenery, confirming Payne's earlier observation as to the efficiency of the Swiss, including in "the arrangement of mountains." He traveled as far north as Lake Lucerne, where he derived the subject matter for a view of the mountains rising above the lake (below right), and as far south as Zermatt, where he took "the train that runs to Gornergrat" to study the famous Matterhorn, the subject of several works in which he used a decorative approach expressive of the charming, playful quality of the mountain's famous quirky shape (opposite).[36] At the same time, he expressed a certain awe of the peak, as demonstrated in *The Matterhorn from Zermatt* (p. 132).[37] Little snow was able to cling to this mountain's sheer walls, and in this work Payne captured the patchwork pattern that resulted, using short, angular strokes suggestive of the strata of the rock face and the snow gathering in its lines and cracks. Centering the north face of the mountain in his composition, Payne accentuated its striking silhouette; while showing the concentrated force of sunlight on the mountain, he conveyed its transcendence by evoking the association often made between the Matterhorn and the Egyptian obelisk.[38]

Among Payne's other subjects at this time were Spiez Castle, on the south bank of the Thunersee (Lake Thun), which he depicted in *Swiss Village [Spiez Castle on Lake Thun]* (p. 133), a painting featuring the square tower of the Romanesque Schlosskirche (founded in 900–1000). Tipping the picture plane

forward, he guides the viewer over the rooftops to this church tower, which in rising over the water connects the human with the spiritual realm of the misty mountains above.[39] In *Mountains in Switzerland* (pp. 134–135), Payne's handling is more vigorous and loose, but he similarly found in this scene a sense of man's deference to nature: the houses set in the contours of the land curve as if to genuflect toward the mountains, with the onion-shaped dome of the Kloster Engelberg, a Benedictine abbey founded in 1120, drawing the viewer's attention upward to the highest of the peaks. Payne's image evokes William

Lake Lucerne, c. 1923. Photographer unknown.
Courtesy of DeRu's Fine Arts

Opposite: *The Matterhorn from Zermatt*, c. 1923. Oil on canvas, 52½ x 48 in. Collection of Mr. and Mrs. Jon R. Stuart

Above: *Swiss Village [Spiez Castle on Lake Thun]*, c. 1923. Oil on canvas, 28 x 34 in. Collection of Mr. and Mrs. Jon R. Stuart

Mountains in Switzerland, c. 1922–1923. Oil on canvas, 28 x 34 in.
Courtesy of DeRu's Fine Arts

Edgar Payne in the Swiss Alps, 1923. Photographer unknown.
Courtesy of DeRu's Fine Arts

Wordsworth's poem "Engelberg, the Hill of Angels," in which the angels' singing in the church turns them into "Visitants" among the clouds.

While Payne may have taken advantage of the high mountain railways in and near Interlaken that transported tourists and mountain climbers to scenic points and trailheads, he also hiked in the mountains.[40] A photograph portrays him heading off on such a venture, wearing woolen attire and a beret and carrying a box of art supplies (opposite). In his entry on *Sunlit Peak, Wellhorn, near Meiringen* (below right) in the catalogue for Payne's 1926 exhibition at the Stendahl Galleries, Anderson stated: "the artist made a laborious climb of 2,000 feet to paint this imposing picture, for the Wellhorn held for him an allure not to be resisted at any cost."[41] To reach some of his sites, Payne also engaged the help of "native guides," as was noted in *California Graphic* in 1926.[42] In addition to the Wellhorn, his subjects during this part of his trip included the Wetterhorn, the Eiger, the Jungfrau, and other peaks in the Bernese Alps.[43] The Jungfrau, or "the Maiden"—its name derived from the once held belief that the peak's summit would never be surmounted and thus would remain forever virginal—was the subject of two Payne paintings. One of these, *Grandeur des Alpes—La Jungfrau,* was included in his exhibition of March 15–April 1, 1924, at the Galeries Jacques Seligmann et fils in Paris; the other, *Le Monarque des Oberland (La Jungfrau),* was shown at the Paris Salon of 1924. Of these, one is undoubtedly the painting titled *The Jungfrau* (p. 138) in the current exhibition. The work marks a change in Payne's handling of Alpine scenes. Pressing the forms of the mountain against the picture plane and using broadly evident gestural strokes, he created a dynamic

and direct image, expressing the powerful nature of a mountain renowned for "appalling precipices, dangerous crevasses, and well-nigh constant falls of hundreds of tons of rock and ice."[44] Another view of the Jungfrau appears in Payne's *The Valley Village* (p. 139). Here the village settlement is more precarious, situated on a steep decline from which the dramatic thrust of the mountain, expressed also through the energy of Payne's brushwork, is made apparent.

Sunlit Peak, Wellhorn, near Meiringen, 1926.
Photograph from Stendahl Galleries catalog.
Courtesy of DeRu's Fine Arts

The Jungfrau, 1923–1924. Oil on canvas, 62 x 62 in. Collection of Paul and Kathleen Bagley

The Valley Village, 1923. Oil on canvas on board, 29 x 29 in. Collection of Thomas T. Tatum

PARIS AND BRITTANY
(SEPTEMBER 1923–JULY 1924)

In late September 1923, the Paynes returned to Paris, where they remained until Evelyn's school year ended in June. Rather than stay in a hotel, the family rented an apartment at 48, rue Vavin, on the Left Bank, while Payne established a studio at 51, boulevard Saint-Jacques, also on the Left Bank. With Evelyn at boarding school, Edgar and Elsie were able to go out in the evenings. They attended performances at the Folies Bergère and the Moulin Rouge and frequented the Café du Dôme in Montparnasse, the gathering place for famous writers including Ernest Hemingway, Ezra Pound, Sinclair Lewis, and Ford Madox Ford. The Paynes' social life, however, centered primarily on old friends. Their main companions were the commercial artist George Evans and his wife, Alma, both of whom Payne knew from Chicago.[45] The two couples spent New Year's Eve at the Café du Dôme along with others of Paris's international artist community, in which Payne now felt at ease.[46]

In contrast with his first visit, when Payne had professed not to care so much for the city, he now became fully absorbed in its art life. His feeling of belonging no doubt stemmed from a significant event that had taken place the previous May, when two of his paintings were exhibited at the Paris Salon of 1923, *Le Grand Pic Blanc* (p. 116) and *Les Haut Sierra [High Sierra]* (p. 88), both measuring forty-three inches square.[47] With the Alpine scene's white glow contrasting with the more tonal Sierra image—rendered in cool lavenders and pale greens—the display of the two works revealed that Payne had indeed conquered the subject of mountains, beyond those of a particular region. Although only his Mont Blanc scene received an honorable mention, both paintings were hung together in the awards section of the exhibition, where painter Jessie Arms Botke reported seeing them.[48] Payne's participation in the Salon was also noticed by a wider press. The *New York Times* stated that the 75 paintings by fifty American artists included among the 4,500 paintings in the exhibition seemed like a small number, but that it was large when one considered "that admission to the Salon represented almost the highest honor to which French painters can aspire and that the judges who pass on entries are exclusively French." Among the few American exhibitors mentioned in the article, Payne was misidentified as "Edward Allen Payne," and it was noted that he, along with William P. Silva, presented California subjects, overlooking Payne's Mont Blanc view.[49] Payne was also the first of only four foreign artists cited in the review of the Salon in the *Paris Telegram,* which reported, "There are a number of works by Americans and English among those shown, such as Mr. Edgar Payne's two beautiful landscapes which are well hung and stand out clear and strong."[50]

Another letter Payne sent home was published in the *Los Angeles Times* on December 30. Although he stated that Paris was "very dark and gloomy" just then, his enthusiasm for the city was evident. Describing his working life, he noted that the light was "still good for painting from about 10 a.m. to 3:30 or 4 p.m." and that he not only "managed to keep busy" but "had his hands full." Acknowledging that Paris was undoubtedly "the real center for artists from all parts to congregate," he described the different artistic types he encountered, including the "freakish tribe, who resort to all sorts of manners and costumes to draw attention to themselves," as well as the serious painters, who in turn gave him many "inducements for serious endeavor." Far more open-minded than he had been during his first stay in the city, he wrote, "Much is to be gained from the moderns as well as the conservatives." He mentioned that he had visited the Autumn Salon (Salon d'Automne), the display of "the wild boys," and observed that considerable interest was "being shown toward America, art and artists throughout Europe."[51] Payne also found his place within the American artist community abroad, joining the American Art Association of Paris, formed in the fall of 1923. He attended a dinner given by the Comité France-Amérique in honor of the new organization and showed two works, *Boats, Chioggia* and *Glacier,* in an exhibition held by the association from January 27 through February 10, 1924.[52]

Shortly after his arrival in Paris, Payne prepared for three additional exhibitions. The first to take place was the *Second Biennial Roman International Exposition,* which opened in late November 1923 and closed in May 1924.[53] Payne stated in his letter, "I have been invited to show and have hung five large canvases in the Biennial at Rome, and was only prevented from a full room by not having time to get enough canvases ready. The Biennial is an important show and I feel somewhat flattered with the honor."[54] In covering the show, the Paris edition of the *New York Herald* commented that although Italian and Anglo-Saxon artists figured largely in it, "it contained few exhibits by American artists, as many of those invited to send contributions were not able to do so in time." Payne's several landscapes "in the Trentino and around Venice" were among the few to be singled out.[55] *Art News* reported that "aside from a room given over to the work of the late Elihu Vedder" and a few works "by the artist Payne," America was "only remarkable in the show

by its absence."[56] In a March article in the *Los Angeles Times,* Anderson provided proof that Payne visited the *Biennial:* "Edgar Payne, who is now in Rome, is winning honors in Italy. He had three entries in the Second Biennial International Exhibition at Rome and one of his pictures, 'Barche Veneziane a Chioggia,' has been reproduced in the catalog."[57] From this we can surmise that a fragment of an article from *The Latin Quarter* contained in the Payne archive referred to this trip. It noted that Payne, along with George Evans and Cornelius Botke (a Dutch-born California artist whom Payne had also known in Chicago and who was the husband of artist Jessie Arms Botke), had "left Thursday on a painting trip through Italy. They will be gone for several weeks."[58]

Payne also contributed to the Venice International Exhibition, which opened in early 1924.[59] At the same time, he kept up appearances in America, sending his two Salon paintings to the Art Institute of Chicago's *Twenty-Eighth Annual Exhibition by Artists of Chicago and Vicinity.* Yet Payne's most significant exhibition, shared with American sculptor Nancy Cox-McCormack, was held in March and April at the Galeries Jacques Seligmann et fils in Paris.[60] Payne had shown jointly with McCormack at the Palette & Chisel Club in Chicago in 1914, so this show was a reunion. Among those who attended the opening were Myron Herrick, the American ambassador to France; the noted collector Mrs. E. H. Harriman (Mary Williamson Averell); and Mrs. Harriman's daughter, Mary Rumsey, whose husband was the sculptor Charles Cary Rumsey. They appeared in a photograph with Payne and McCormack alongside a bust of Mussolini that McCormack had created from life in 1923 and that was included in the show (p. 142).[61]

The exhibition took place during a transitional time for the Seligmann gallery, which since its opening in 1904 had served an illustrious group of American and European collectors as well as museums. At the end of October 1923, the gallery's owner, Jacques Seligmann, died and his son Germain, a writer and scholar, who had been running the New York branch of the gallery, took over its management.[62] An article in the Payne archive notes that it was in fact Germain who arranged the Payne-McCormack exhibition: "M. Germain Seligman, to whom we are indebted for the revelation of these two fine talents, and who in this way has been faithful to [Jacques Seligmann's] sympathies always manifested towards American art, intends to renew the experiment, and to offer from time to time hospitality in his luxurious salons to American artists."[63] The

Paris—Evening Telegraph stated: "Mr. Payne is the first modern painter who has been permitted to show in this gallery, one of the most beautiful in Paris."[64]

At the Seligmann gallery, Payne exhibited sixteen works, including at least one image of the Sierra Nevada, one of the Monterey coast, one of his views of the Jungfrau, and scenes of Adriatic boats and the French and Swiss Alps.[65] Among the works, *Haut Sommet* was possibly *The Matterhorn from Zermatt,* which was reproduced on the catalogue's cover, although it was titled *Borne de Frontière (Mont Cervin)* in a review.[66] The painting titled *Neiges Éternelles—Mont Blanc* was, no doubt, *The Great White Peak [Mt. Blanc, France]* (p. 145). Just as Payne felt more confident as an artist in Paris on his second visit to the city, his approach in this painting reflects a new self-assurance. Here, working

Exhibition Opening, n.d. Photographer unknown. Courtesy of DeRu's Fine Arts. From left: Mrs. Charles Cary Rumsey (Mary), Edgar Payne, Myron Herrick, bust of Benito Mussolini by Nancy Cox-McCormack, Nancy Cox-McCormack, unknown man, Mrs. E. H. Harriman

from an oil sketch pinned to his canvas, which can be seen in the photograph of Payne in his Paris studio (p. 144), he adhered more closely to the actual profile of the mountain than he had in *Le Grand Pic Blanc,* featuring the contours of the massif more accurately but utilizing a new method of applying paint. Instead of painting in layers, he used a rhythmic application of broken, stitchlike strokes, a technique that increases the action of the viewer's eye and results in a sensation of greater light. While Payne's method suggests that of the French and Italian Divisionists, it also derives from his own trajectory toward directness and succinctness. Here, as his title suggests, he focuses on the peak's whiteness as its primary distinguishing aspect. He would explain the understanding behind such an approach in *Composition of Outdoor Painting,* stating that in broadly painted pictures, "the viewer must use his imagination" in order to feel the "abstract impression as intended by the artist."[67] Payne enhanced the viewer's experience of such an impression by making the foreground and sky darker than in his earlier Mont Blanc painting, while his similar stitches of paint in the sky create a subtle light that adds to the overall shimmering effect. Payne would not use such a handling to this extent again, which suggests that this painting was a culmination of his Alpine experience and one he therefore would not repeat.

Reviews in American and French newspapers of Payne's show were universally complimentary. Many critics remarked on Payne's modernity and observed that he had merged a decorative and a powerful style of painting. Several noted that he painted in a strong and vital way that was well suited to the grandeur of his subjects and that in rendering mountains he had dominated them, depicting them with an American sort of

breadth. A commentary in *La revue moderne illustrée des arts et de la vie* stated that to obtain the effects of grandiosity in his views of the "Alpes de Savoie," Payne had conquered the formidable mountains by omitting detail and using strong colors and a firm brush.[68] In its Paris report, *Art News* noted that Payne's "landscapes have a very uncommon breadth and a richness rarely met with."[69] The Paris edition of the *New York Herald* pronounced that Payne's mountains were "real, rugged, and colorful."[70] Payne's scenes of Italian boats also drew notice. One reviewer remarked on how these scenes were filled with believable movement and color, yet demonstrated control.[71]

On May 1, exactly one month after Payne's Seligmann show closed, the Paris Salon opened. Payne's contribution consisted of two paintings: *Le Monarque des Oberland (La Jungfrau)* and *Les Hauteurs,* the latter a view of the Wellhorn.[72] According to *The Latin Quarter,* this time the selection jury had been severe, refusing "well known artists who have exhibited for years."[73] Thus, it was no doubt gratifying to Payne to have his works accepted. However, a new method of installation caused consternation. Instead of grouping works by subject, as in the past, organizers separated foreign art from that of the French artists so that foreign visitors could find works by artists of their own nationalities. This arrangement was unsatisfactory to foreign and French artists alike, who, the *New York Times* noted, held the view that "art . . . is international and has always been regarded as international in the salon, as elsewhere."[74] Paris's *Le Figaro* cited the location of Payne's "mountain scenes" facing a portrait by the Polish painter Boleslas Jan Czedekowski as illustrative of the odd juxtapositions resulting from such sequestering.[75]

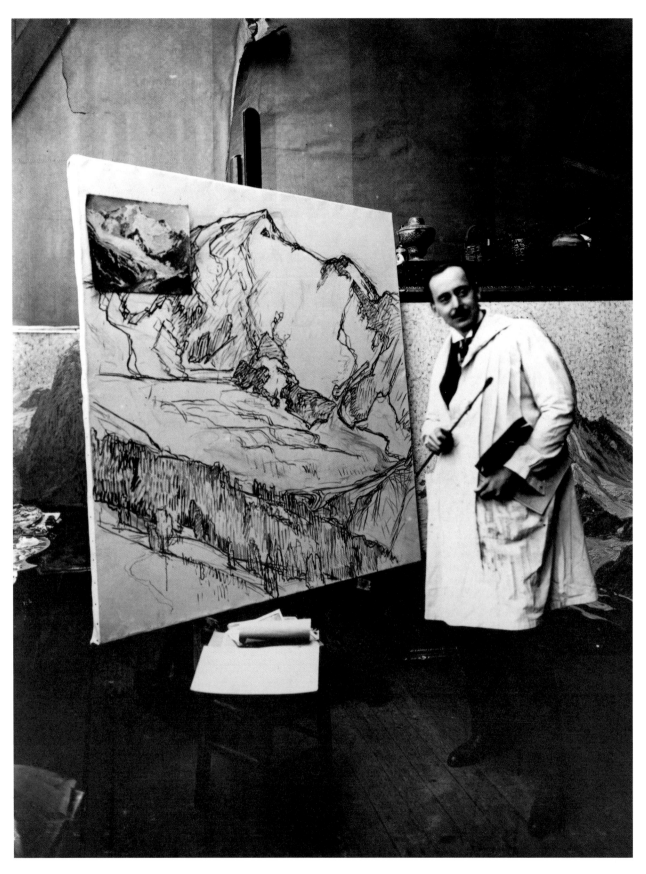

Edgar Payne in his Paris studio with *The Great White Peak [Mt. Blanc, France]*, 1924. Photographer unknown.
Courtesy of DeRu's Fine Arts

The Great White Peak [Mt. Blanc, France], 1924. Oil on canvas, 62 x 62 in. Los Angeles County Museum of Art. Gift of James N. and Linda S. Ries in memory of Harold and Dorothy Shrier, M.2000.181. Digital image © 2009 Museum Associates / LACMA / Art Resource, NY

Château de Montrésor [Loire Valley, France], c. 1924. Oil on canvas, 29 x 29 in. Collection of Betty Goldfield

In the spring, when the school year ended for Evelyn, the Paynes drove in a new direction. Heading south, they traveled through the Loire Valley before turning northwest into Brittany. Along the way they visited ancient castles, which Payne sketched, captivated by the strength of their forms and their endurance (below right). Among the works to follow from this trip, *Château de Montrésor [Loire Valley, France]* (opposite) depicts a castle in Touraine, built initially in the Middle Ages and rebuilt in the Renaissance. Payne's vantage point from below reveals his respect for the subsistence of this powerful stone fortress, which still towered over the street. The entry for this painting in the catalogue for Payne's 1926 Stendahl Galleries exhibition described it as a "beautiful picture, glowing with subdued color."[76] Payne's approach was similar in his other depictions of medieval castles.[77]

In choosing Brittany as a destination, Payne followed many other American artists who had been a presence in the region since the 1860s, when a group led by the American expatriate Robert Wylie formed an artists' colony in Pont-Aven. Brittany's sunlit beaches, lush fields, jagged coastline, and ancient harbors attracted the attention of artists, but many were also drawn to the Breton fisherfolk and their colorful and distinctive traditional attire. Payne also found this aspect of Brittany compelling. Whereas previously the figure had not been significant in his work, he spent much of his time rendering this subject in the fishing ports of Concarneau and Douarnenez. This interest is revealed in Payne's many drawings of the clothing and poses of men and women (p. 149). Evelyn Payne Hatcher recalled:

Dad's sketches are mostly of fishermen, and you can see what they wore in the following sketches. The color of the main garments were, in Concarneau, mostly what is still called "Breton red," often very patched. The caps were large navy berets. In France the edge of the beret was always tucked under, not worn outside as sometimes seen in this country, and in Brittany the front was pulled forward to shade the eyes.[78]

While Payne was attracted to the continuity with the past that the fisherfolk represented, he also used figures as compositional elements, at times taking

Château on the Way to Brittany, n.d. Pencil on paper, 10 x 10 in. Courtesy of DeRu's Fine Arts

Breton Fishermen Unloading Fish, c. 1928. Photograph by Edgar Payne. Courtesy of DeRu's Fine Arts

photographs in which he selected his angles carefully to bring out rhythmically organized groupings of men and nautical forms (opposite). In *Unloading Fish, Concarneau* (p. 170), depicting a casual scene of daily life, his staging abilities are evident in the single curving line that draws together figures and boats. In *Fishermen's Wives Bargaining, Breton Scene, Concarneau* (pp. 150–151), the women and men on the dock blend in with their surroundings yet serve to structure the arrangement.

As in Chioggia, boats were Payne's primary focus in Brittany. Elsie recalled, "We went mad over those Breton scenes . . . I painted the villages and the quaint houses, and left the boats to Edgar."[79] Payne became familiar with all aspects of the boats, as he had in Italy, by drawing, making "color notes," sketches, and complete studies (p. 153). His fascination with the construction of the boats even led him to make models of them after his return to America. Elegantly detailed and measuring four feet in length, these were produced before plastic parts could be purchased, and thus Payne enlisted the help of his friend the dentist George Brandriff, who made his drill available. In turn, Payne gave Brandriff, a "Sunday painter," painting lessons; Brandriff eventually quit dentistry to pursue a career in art. Elsie even played a role in the production by making boats' sails (p. 153).[80] In photographs that Payne took of Brittany boats, he again considered their arrangements, with an eye to their relationships with shapes along the shoreline of hills and buildings (p. 152).

Payne was fascinated by the particular facets of the boats he observed, and those of Brittany were quite different from those of the Adriatic. Instead of having lateen sails, they were rigged fore and aft, their sails set along the line of the keel rather than

perpendicular to it. This flexibility enabled mariners to adjust the sails for the rough seas of the Atlantic as well as for the calmer waters of the English Channel. In his paintings, Payne depicted both the small, single-masted sardine sloops, fitted with boards along their keels so they could be raised and lowered depending on the conditions of the harbor, and the larger two-masted tuna yawls, which were arrayed with multiple sails. Arranging the varied forms of the boats as would a composer or choreographer, Payne sought to lead viewers through his arrangements and at the same time achieve compositional harmony, which manifested his belief that such organizing rhythms are a

Sketches of Breton Fishermen, n.d. Pencil on paper, 10 x 8 in. Courtesy of DeRu's Fine Arts

Fishermen's Wives Bargaining, Breton Scene, Concarneau, 1924.
Oil on canvas, 32 x 42 in. Payton Family Collection

Tuna Yawls, Brittany, France, c. 1924. Photograph by Edgar Payne. Courtesy of DeRu's Fine Arts

Left: *Model of Breton Tuna Boat (Yawl)*,
c. 1925. Painted wood and metal,
44 x 34 x 12 in. Collection of Mark
Sauer

Below: *Tuna Boats, Concarneau*, c. 1924.
Pencil on paper, 8 x 10 in. Courtesy
of DeRu's Fine Arts

Tuna Fisherman, Concarneau, c. 1924. Oil on canvas, 29 x 29 in. Collection of Mr. and Mrs. Thomas B. Stiles II

human necessity in visual art as well as other art forms (pp. 154, 156–157). The designs of Payne's Brittany paintings reveal the sophistication and confidence that he had gained over the course of his trip. This is evident in a comparison of his earlier *Cargo Boats, Chioggia, Italy* (p. 129) with his *Breton Tuna Boats, Concarneau, France* (pp. 164–165). Both follow a compositional type he would identify as the radiating line in *Composition of Outdoor Painting,* but in the Brittany scene he loosened his compositional structure, encouraging viewers to move in and out among the boats in a slow, lingering manner that emphasizes an enjoyment of their forms. Only after prolonged gazing does it become clear that the artist arranged the boats' angles to gently guide his audience.

America and Europe (July 1924–1928)

At the end of the summer, the Paynes began their homeward journey, traveling by way of London. After a delay of two weeks caused by an injury Evelyn incurred while playing, they returned to America on the SS *Leviathan.*[81] Instead of going directly to California, they stopped off in Chicago, where they remained for several months. In February and March, Payne again participated in the Art Institute of Chicago's annual *Artists of Chicago and Vicinity* exhibition, showing *Bernese Peaks* and *Tuna Fishermen,* the latter perhaps the painting in the present exhibition titled *Tuna Fisherman, Concarneau* (opposite).[82] Anderson reported in an article of March 29, 1925, that at the time Payne was still in Chicago, the Newcomb Macklin & Co. galleries were holding an exhibition of his work that consisted almost entirely of European scenes.[83] Payne also showed *Sails of Cameret* [*sic*], a Brittany image, at the 1925 annual

exhibition of the Pennsylvania Academy of the Fine Arts, Philadelphia, which took place in February. In October, his *Peaks and Shadows,* a view of Kandersteg, Bern, Switzerland, won the "best landscape" award at the *Sixteenth Annual Exhibition of the California Art Club* at the Los Angeles Museum of History, Science, and Art.[84]

Delayed by a car accident in Denver, in which no injuries were incurred, the Paynes returned in late May to Los Angeles, where Anderson reported that Payne had brought with him a carload of canvases from his "three short and busy years in France, Italy, and Switzerland." Anderson stated, "Payne is glad to be back. No place like California. A platitude— and how true."[85] Although Neeta Marquis wrote in the *Los Angeles Times* in November that Payne was preparing his work for an exhibition to be held at the Biltmore Salon,[86] he would not show his art at this venue until June 1929; the first display of his art after his return occurred that month in Chicago at the Thomas Whipple Dunbar Galleries. A reviewer for the *Chicago Evening Post* reported that the exhibition "represented some of the best work brought back to this country," concluding with the comment, "It is a brilliant exhibition as a whole."[87] Nonetheless, the premier showcase for Payne's European efforts consisted of the spring 1926 exhibition of his work held at the Stendahl Galleries, of which fifty of the sixty paintings included were European subjects; two boat models were also on view. The exhibition was accompanied by a catalogue with a biography and appreciation and entries on the works by Anderson, an essay by Hogue, and fifty-one halftone illustrations, only four of which depicted California subjects. Lauding the show, the critics felt it demonstrated Payne's "full work" and

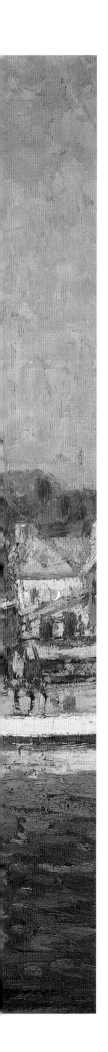

growth as an artist, revealing not only that he was a "master of color and technique" but also that he had "transformed his canvases into poems of color." Hogue commented that while Payne's Salon honor was an achievement received by few, "the canvases which he brought back from three years in the Swiss and French Alps and in the Adriatic and Mediterranean seas and off the coast of Brittany give testimony of a mature art that merits the appellation 'master.'"[88] Arthur Millier observed in Payne's images of boats that the artist had "reacted to life as a moving and colorful pageant" while drawing "a great many picturesque details together into bold and colorful masses."[89] Another critic remarked how Payne, in omitting anything "hasty or superficial from his work," revealed his understanding of the "art of making a picture."[90]

Despite the welcome Payne received from his supporters in California, who no doubt believed that his return was permanent, in October 1926 he abruptly moved to Westport, Connecticut.[91] Payne biographer Rena Coen suggests that Payne decided to move east at that time to expand on his successes in Chicago and California. Yet, if this was the case, he made little headway in the New York art world, exhibiting his work in this period only at the Women's Town Improvement Association in the Westport YMCA.[92]

Leaving the East Coast at the end of April 1927, Payne returned to Los Angeles, where another exhibition of his work at the Stendahl Galleries included mainly European subjects. Sonia Wolfson started her review of the show with the remark, "To take a vicarious trip to Europe no more discerning guide than Edgar Alwyn [sic] Payne is conceivable." At the end of her commentary, she alluded to what may have been on the minds of many of Payne's followers in California—that in painting the Alps, Payne had raised an awareness that the Sierra Nevada equaled them in grandeur and beauty, as only painting both ranges could have done. She wrote:

> Completely awed by the impenetrable silence and the vast solid masses of rock structures [in the Alpine views], a sense of poignant longing nevertheless overtakes us, and soon we realize it's sheer homesickness, for the Alps are rivaled in grandeur by our Sierras. With patriotic fervor we then turn to Mr. Payne's "Sierra Twilight" and breathe an unconscious prayer of thanksgiving for the beauties of our homeland and the artists who, knowing the glories of other lands, are big enough to convey them to us and still bring us to a realization of the beauties close to us.[93]

For Payne, these observations must have struck home. That they did so is reflected in Fred Hogue's article "God of the Mountains," in which he recorded Payne's responses to questions regarding the differences between the mountains of Europe and those of California. While exaggerating the scope of Payne's travels, stating that he had painted in "the Swiss Alps, the Bavarian Alps, the French Alps, the Maritime Alps, with side excursions in to the Carpentarian

Brittany Harbor, c. 1924. Oil on canvas, 28 x 34 in. Courtesy of Redfern Gallery

Brittany Boats, c. 1924. Oil on canvas, 30 x 40 in. Robert and Nadine Hall Collection. Image courtesy of Chris Bliss

Brittany Boats, c. 1924. Oil on canvas, 40 x 50 in. Collection of D. L. Stuart Jr.

Brittany Boats, c. 1924. Oil on canvas, 28 x 34 in. Private collection

The Race, 1922. Oil on canvas, 28 x 34 in. Private collection. Courtesy of Trotter Galleries

and Vosges Mountains, and the Pyrenèes," Hogue reported that Payne told him he had discovered that these mountains were "tame, domesticated, colorless, compared to the wild vastness of the Sierras of California." Hogue admitted that he felt humiliated at having little knowledge of his own country when he learned from Payne that there were "more mountain lakes within 200 miles of Monmoth in Mono county, California, than in the whole of Europe." To Hogue's protest that the Alps had a glow lacking in the Sierra, as "under our warmer skies, the snow leaves the slopes of the mountains and is only to be found in the canyons," Payne replied with "an amused gaze" that made Hogue "uncomfortable." Hogue felt that Payne was "marveling at the valor of [the critic's] ignorance that the glow of the Alps was a cloud rather than a snow effect," and that during a summer spent in the Swiss Alps, Payne had seen such a glow only twice, yet he had not made a single trip to the Sierra without seeing it.

When Hogue pressed Payne for more particulars as to his preference for the Sierra over the Alps, Payne stated that "when one goes into the Swiss Alps . . . he does not get the feeling of communion with nature that one experiences here in California." Payne went on to note that he found more color and atmosphere in the High Sierra than in the Alps and that whereas the Alps were a uniform gray color of granite, the mixture of granite and pumice in the Sierra, along with the mineral ledges to be found everywhere, resulted in a diversity of color, including "reds and greens not to be found anywhere in Europe." He stated, "One finds here the mountains of Switzerland under the skies of Italy." After experiencing the Alps, Payne could also claim that the Sierra Nevada was underappreciated.

He noted that he had stood on the banks of "fifty mountain lakes that are neither charted nor named" and had "sketched in the shadow of mountains that would be famous in Europe, but that are known here only as units of the Sierra range." To Hogue, such comments implied that Payne's European travels had served the purpose of enabling him to settle down and concentrate on the beauty of California. After commending Payne's views of Mediterranean villages and Breton castles, he concluded, "But what impressed me most is that, after covering half the circumference of the earth, he has returned to California, convinced that our own Sierras possess a greater appeal to the artist, the nature lover, the lover of the romantic, the beautiful and the sublime, than aught an alien clime can offer."[94] In the years ahead, Payne would renew his commitment to painting the Sierra, resuming his drives into the mountains and his camping expeditions, at times bringing students. More aware of the distinctive traits of the Sierra than he had been before his travels to Europe, he expressed their rugged and glowing aspects with renewed vigor, creating images full of life that further enhanced his reputation.

Even after returning to Sierra subjects, pride in his European paintings led Payne to continue to promote them. Several were on view in his June–July show at the galleries of the Chicago Galleries Association, and he included images of Adriatic and Breton fishing boats among the eight decorative paintings he created for the lobby of the new Hotel St. Paul, Los Angeles. Payne also focused on European subject matter while convalescing from pneumonia in the Bronx in the fall of 1927, when he used Elsie's tempera materials to produce small paintings, including Alpine views, from his European sketches.

In January 1928, Payne had a joint exhibition with Dedrick Stuber at the Wilshire Galleries in Los Angeles, in which his scenes of the High Sierra, the Alps, and European fishing boats were described as "decorative pictures that are so well-known and well-liked that there is no need to describe them here."[95] The show was a success, and that summer the Paynes returned to Europe on the proceeds. In making this return trip, Payne may have been motivated more by commercial reasons than by a desire for conquest. As Anderson noted, the artist told him that he preferred to paint the "more romantic, more colorful Southwest" but that the local market was not worth painting for, as its "percentage of art illiteracy is the highest in two continents."[96] The family departed on the SS *Minnekahda* on June 9, 1928.[97] An itinerary of their trip does not exist, but the family probably disembarked in Bolougne-sur-Mer, France, and from there traveled along the coast to Concarneau. That they also returned to Chioggia on this sojourn suggests that the trip's primary objective was gathering material for boat paintings,[98] and Payne made ample use of his camera to this end, as Jean Stern details in his essay in this catalogue. The family, however, also spent time on the Riviera, as Payne registered a Model T Ford with the Préfet du département d'Alpes Maritimes in Nice, France, on July 24, 1928.[99] George Brandriff's widow recorded a visit by her husband with the Paynes in Brittany at the end of the summer.[100] They returned home on the *Minnekahda,* leaving on September 15 from Boulogne-sur-Mer and reaching New York on September 24.[101]

After his return to America, Payne did not again venture to Europe, although he built on the success of the works that resulted from these trips. He continued to exhibit them as well as paint new scenes of the Alps and European fishing craft. In many of these paintings he repeated elements of earlier works, creating weaker variations of them that stand in contrast with the vitality of those he created both during his trips abroad and directly after his return.

Conclusion

Among Payne's objectives in going to Europe was to prove that his dexterity and skill were not limited to rendering Sierra Nevada and Southern California scenes. He not only accomplished this quest but also enhanced his reputation overall. The trip also afforded him the chance to validate his efforts in painting the Sierra, which in turn renewed his energies in rendering them upon his return. Thus, he may have felt that his European adventure was an artistic challenge now met, but not his life's work. Nonetheless, despite his disparagement of the Alps after his return to America, he had not compromised in painting them, as noted by Sonia Wolfson, but instead expressed his reverence for the grander manifestations of nature evident in their dramatic and picturesque forms in his art. In his views of fishing boats, he conveyed his respect for the endurance of these ancient vessels while using form and color to engage the viewer in the distinctive experience of each scene, carrying out his conviction that "painting is the art of thinking."[102] Over the course of his European odyssey, Payne, of course, did not manage to paint all of Europe's paintable things. Nonetheless, he brought out the beauty, vitality, and nobility in his subjects that transcended their visual appearances, conquering Europe in his own way.

Breton Tuna Boats, Concarneau, France, c. 1924. Oil on canvas, 40 x 50 in. Private collection

Fishing Boats, Concarneau, c. 1924. Oil on canvas, 33 x 43 in. Private collection

The Homeport, Concarneau, c. 1924. Oil on canvas, 28 x 34 in. Collection of Paul and Kathleen Bagley

In the Canal, Chioggia, c. 1923. Oil on canvas, 28 x 34 in. Courtesy of William A. Karges Fine Art

Italian Boats at Harbor, c. 1923. Oil on canvas, 28 x 34 in. Payton Family Collection

Unloading Fish, Concarneau, c. 1924. Oil on canvas, 24 x 28 in. The Edward H. and Yvonne J. Boseker Collection

NOTES

1. This quote is from an unsourced article of 1921, probably by art critic Antony Anderson, in which the author writes that seeing one of Payne's canvases led him "to envision [the artist] struggling upward, scorched by the sun at noonday and chilled by the frosts of early morning, but steadily approaching his ideal, the summit of the mountain. His chafed feet are bleeding and his brain reels, but he perseveres for he is a true artist. Finally he scales the topmost ledges, stands in solitary triumph in the great alone, higher than the eagle's nest or vultures soar; above the lightnings that shiver a giant pine in a canyon far below. There and there alone could he find the blending of light and shade, the cloud effects and the transparency of certain colors in so rarefied an atmosphere with which he has produced what is perhaps the strongest, most vigorous study of the California High Sierras ever painted . . . Others have stood at [the] base [of the Sierra] and sketched them in towering majesty. He is one of the hardy few who have reached the summit." Edgar and Elsie Palmer Payne Papers, DeRu's Fine Arts, Bellflower, CA.

2. Vandyke Brown [Antony Anderson], "Los Angeles Letter," *Life and Art* 9 (June 2, 1922). Anderson wrote under this pseudonym from 1920 to 1922. See Nancy Dustin Wall Moure, *A History of the Laguna Beach Art Association to 1935* (Los Angeles: Dustin Publications, 1999), 20n26. Edgar and Elsie Palmer Payne Papers, DeRu's Fine Arts, Bellflower, CA.

3. Antony Anderson, Of Art and Artists, *Los Angeles Times,* April 22, 1923. Edgar and Elsie Palmer Payne Papers, DeRu's Fine Arts, Bellflower, CA.

4. Edgar A. Payne, *Composition of Outdoor Painting* (Hollywood, CA: Seward, 1941); repr., 7th ed., ed. DeRu's Fine Arts with addenda by Evelyn Payne Hatcher (Bellflower, CA: DeRu's Fine Arts, 2005). Page references are to the 1941 edition.

5. "Edgar Alwin Payne: Artist Was Known for Paintings of Alps and Sierras," *New York Times,* April 9, 1947.

6. Fred Hogue, "The God of the Mountains," *Los Angeles Times,* May 22, 1927; also Fred Hogue, "Grandeur of California Sierras: Paints Sunset Glow and Morning Light," *Hemet (CA) News,* July 1, 1927. Edgar and Elsie Palmer Payne Papers, DeRu's Fine Arts, Bellflower, CA.

7. This organization was begun in 1905 under the patronage of Auguste Rodin, the novelist Paul Adam, and the composer Vincent d'Indy. The invitation Payne received stated that his last exhibition had brought him to the union's attention and that he was among one hundred others asked to join that year. Letter, Union internationale des beaux-arts et des lettres, 1913. Edgar and Elsie Palmer Payne Papers, DeRu's Fine Arts, Bellflower, CA.

8. "Tribute Paid Noted Artist," *Los Angeles Times,* May 23, 1922. Edgar and Elsie Palmer Payne Papers, DeRu's Fine Arts, Bellflower, CA.

9. Anderson, Of Art and Artists, May 28, 1922. Edgar and Elsie Palmer Payne Papers, DeRu's Fine Arts, Bellflower, CA.

10. The others on the list are William Alanson Bryan, Howard Russell Butler (on a stay in Los Angeles that lasted from 1920 to 1926), Val J. Costello, Edward S. Curtis (the noted photographer of Native American subjects), Fred B. Foster, H. C. Franklin, Benjamin B. Hampton, Alfred Isaacson, Thomas J. Orbison, Edouard A. Vysekal, Rob Wagner, Max Wieczorek, and a few others whose names are not fully legible.

11. This exhibition was held in the Fine Arts Building on Michigan Avenue.

12. An automobile license issued to Payne on August 22, 1922, listed his address as 21, rue d'Athènes, the location of this hotel, which has been in existence since at least the 1880s and is now known as the Hôtel ATN. Edgar and Elsie Palmer Payne Papers, DeRu's Fine Arts, Bellflower, CA.

13. Noted in Neeta Marquis, "Southland Artist Holds Paris Exhibit," *Los Angeles Times,* November 22, 1925. Edgar and Elsie Palmer Payne Papers, DeRu's Fine Arts, Bellflower, CA.

14. Anderson, Of Art and Artists, November 12, 1922. Edgar and Elsie Palmer Payne Papers, DeRu's Fine Arts, Bellflower, CA.

15. Antony Anderson wrote that the "three mountains that you see on the road to Chamonix" are depicted in *The Mont Blanc Range.* See *Edgar Alwin Payne and His Work,* by Antony Anderson and Fred S. Hogue (Los Angeles: Stendahl Art Galleries, 1926), 45 (no. 28). Edgar and Elsie Palmer Payne Papers, DeRu's Fine Arts, Bellflower, CA.

16. Anderson, Of Art and Artists, November 12, 1922.

17. For information about, and identification of, Payne's sites in the Alps, I would like to thank Jean Pavillard, who has climbed these mountains and whose expertise has been invaluable.

18. This rack-and-pinion railway, operating in the summer, starts from Le Fayet station in the town of Saint-Gervais-les-Bains and reaches the ridge of Mont Forchet, which provides a view of the Aiguille de Bionnassay before descending.

19. Hogue, "God of the Mountains."

20. For example, Lord Byron's dramatic poem *Manfred* (1817) includes the following lines: "Mont Blanc is the monarch of mountains; / They crown'd him long ago / On a throne of rocks, in a robe of clouds, / With a diadem of snow." Percy Bysshe Shelley also paid homage to the mountain in "Mont Blanc: Lines Written in the Vale of Chamouni" (1817), including the lines "Mont Blanc appears,—still, snowy and serene / Its subject mountains their unearthly forms / Pile around it, ice and rock; . . ." See also Samuel Taylor Coleridge, "Hymn Before Sunrise, in the Vale of Chamouni" (1802).

21. Edgar Payne, quoted in Anderson, Of Art and Artists, November 12, 1922.

22. Noted in Edgar A. Payne, "In Switzerland: A Letter Dated 15 de Avril," *Laguna Beach Life,* May 18, 1923. Edgar and Elsie Palmer Payne Papers, DeRu's Fine Arts, Bellflower, CA.

23. Ibid.

24. The Simplon Tunnel, which opened in 1906, was then the longest railway tunnel in the world. Payne wrote that Brig was "a very quaint little village, with old chateau and church, the latter with its funny little tower top, shaped, as Mark Twain says, 'like an inverted turnip.' However, this particular church goes him one better, as the tower has a row of windows shaped like inverted keyholes." Ibid. This structure was probably the Stockalperschloss, a castle built between 1651 and 1671.

25. Payne, "In Switzerland."

26. While in Geneva, Payne probably gathered material for *Peaks of Tonnay.* See Anderson and Hogue, *Payne and His Work,* 47 (no. 30).

27. For this part of Payne's journey, see Rena Neumann Coen, *The Paynes, Edgar & Elsie: American Artists* (Minneapolis, MN: Payne Studios, 1988), 37.

28. Coen remarked that the couple had come into contact with a large group of compatriots. Ibid., 37.

29. See Richard J. Goy, *Chioggia and the Villages of the Venetian Lagoon: Studies in Urban History* (Cambridge: Cambridge University Press, 1985).

30. Evelyn Payne Hatcher, "Planning Compositions," in *The Drawings of Edgar Payne, 1883–1947,* with introduction by Jean Stern (Minneapolis, MN: Payne Studios, 2002), 15. Payne also created a number of scenes of boats in Sottomarina on the Gulf of Venice, a commune of Chioggia, to which it is connected by a bridge. See Anderson and Hogue, *Payne and His Work,* 25 (no. 8), 41 (no. 24), and 50 (no. 33).

31. S. Fred Hogue, "The Art of Edgar Alwyn [sic] Payne," *Los Angeles Times,* May 23, 1926. Edgar and Elsie Palmer Payne Papers, DeRu's Fine Arts, Bellflower, CA.

32. I would like to thank Gilberto Penzo, historian of Venetian boats and boatbuilder, for his identification of Payne's Adriatic boats. For information about the boats, I also consulted H. Warington Smyth, *Mast and Sail in Europe and Asia* (London: John Murray, 1906), 231–286. I would like to thank Simon Chiu for bringing this source to my attention.

33. Payne, *Composition of Outdoor Painting,* 59.

34. Elizabeth Robins Pennell, "Venetian Boats," *Harper's New Monthly Magazine* 80 (March 1890), 554–555.

35. Coen, *Paynes, Edgar & Elsie,* 40. This hotel still exists.

36. Mentioned in Anderson and Hogue, *Payne and His Work,* 45 (no. 28).

37. Payne's vantage point in this work was probably Zmutt, a small village west of Zermatt, from which the north face of the mountain is in view. I would like to thank Jean Pavillard for his help in identifying Payne's viewpoint.

38. This connection was made by John Ruskin. See *Selections from the Writings of John Ruskin* (New York: John Wiley and Sons, 1868), 20.

39. Payne's view of the castle is visible from the platform of the Spiez railway station, suggesting that he may have sketched this scene in passing.

40. Payne could have taken the Wengernalp Railway from the town of Lauterbrunnen and from there transferred to the Jungfraubahn, the cogwheel railway completed in 1912—then and now the highest train route in Europe. Modeled on the cogwheel railway on New Hampshire's Mount Washington, this train passed through the Eiger tunnel, under the Eiger, and stopped at the Jungfraujoch, in the midst of the glacier. *Muirhead's Switzerland,* a guidebook that Payne may have had in hand, observed that the Jungfraubahn attained a height of more than 11,000 feet, bringing "the most unathletic into the upper regions of the expert climber," and that telescopes were provided at the viewing station. See Findlay Muirhead, ed., *Muirhead's Switzerland: A Guide Book of Switzerland, with the Chamonix and the Italian Lakes* (New York: Macmillan, 1923). Another train ran from Grindelwald to Kleine Scheidegg, from which many trails led into the high country, among them the path down to Wengen, where Payne may have derived his vantage point for painting *The Jungfrau.*

41. Anderson and Hogue, *Payne and His Work,* 48 (no. 31).

42. "California Art Club President Exhibits," *California Graphic,* May 29, 1926. Edgar and Elsie Palmer Payne Papers, DeRu's Fine Arts, Bellflower, CA.

43. Anderson and Hogue, *Payne and His Work: Wellhorn,* 23 (no. 6), 48 (no. 31), 52 (no. 35), and *Wetterhorn,* 26 (no. 9). *The Eiger at Grindelwald* is illustrated in Goldfield Galleries, *Edgar Payne (1882–1947),* with introduction by Edward Goldfield and biography by Nancy Moure (Los Angeles: Goldfield Galleries, 1987), no. 50.

44. John L. Stoddard, "Switzerland," in *Norway, Switzerland, Athens, Venice,* vol. 1 of *John L. Stoddard's Lectures* (Chicago: Shuman, 1912), pt. 2.

45. Coen, *Paynes, Edgar & Elsie,* 40.

46. Ibid., 41.

47. The Salon of 1923 marked the reunion, after thirty-three years, of the Société des artistes français with the more conservative Société nationale des beaux-arts.

48. "Gen. Gourand Meets with Edgar Payne," *Los Angeles Times,* August 7, 1923. Edgar and Elsie Palmer Payne Papers, DeRu's Fine Arts, Bellflower, CA.

49. "Americans Shine in Paris Salon," *New York Times,* May 1, 1923. This article notes that April 30 was "Varnishing Day."

50. *Paris Telegram* [1923]. This publication was in English. Edgar and Elsie Palmer Payne Papers, DeRu's Fine Arts, Bellflower, CA.

51. Edgar Payne, quoted in Anderson, Of Art and Artists, December 30, 1923. Edgar and Elsie Palmer Payne Papers, DeRu's Fine Arts, Bellflower, CA.

52. *American Art Association Exhibition,* Paris, January 27–February 10, 1924. The exhibition was held on the rue Joseph Bara. Edgar and Elsie Palmer Payne Papers, DeRu's Fine Arts, Bellflower, CA.

53. The American section of this exhibition was headed by the sculptor Frederick Triebel, whose efforts were assisted by the prominent American artists Edwin Blashfield, Daniel Chester French, Frederick MacMonnies, George Gray Barnard, and Frederick Dielman. Dielman, commissioner of painting, was in turn aided by the noted painters Frank Benson, Childe Hassam, and Willard Metcalf. While the Roman commissioners were grateful to the Americans for contributing, the Americans, as Triebel pronounced, felt that the "valuable aid" provided by the Romans gave "ample assurance of the importance that the American Section will assume at the coming exposition, of which it is intended to make, above all, the manifestation of the highest class of art production and of the highest trend of art culture." "America to Send Art Exhibit to Rome," *New York Times,* July 15, 1923. See also "Rome to See Our Art," *New York Times,* November 18, 1923.

54. The works he showed were *Sunlit Peaks* (probably the same view of the Wellhorn that he would exhibit in 1926 at the Stendahl Galleries as *Sunlit Peak*), *The High Alps, The Ligurian Coast, Adriatic Boats,* and *Boats of Chioggia.* Edgar Payne, quoted in Anderson, Of Art and Artists, December 30, 1923.

55. The mention of the Trentino was in error. "Rome Art Show Draws Society: Name of Members of American Colony and Visitors to the Eternal City," *New York Herald,* Paris edition, 1924. Edgar and Elsie Palmer Payne Papers, DeRu's Fine Arts, Bellflower, CA.

56. "Few Americans in the Rome Biennial," *Art News* 22 (December 15, 1923): 5.

57. Anderson, Of Art and Artists, March 9, 1924. Anderson misstated the number of Payne's works in the *Biennial:* Payne showed five, not three, paintings. Edgar and Elsie

Palmer Payne Papers, DeRu's Fine Arts, Bellflower, CA.

58. Undated article from *The Latin Quarter*. Edgar and Elsie Palmer Payne Papers, DeRu's Fine Arts, Bellflower, CA.

59. Payne stated in his letter that he was getting a canvas ready for this exhibition. See Anderson, Of Art and Artists, December 30, 1923.

60. The best source on McCormack is the introduction in Nancy Cox-McCormack and Lawrence S. Rainey, "Ezra Pound in the Paris Years," *Sewanee Review* 102 (Winter 1994): 93–95. Payne's exhibition was titled *Exposition de peintures par Edgar Alwin Payne*.

61. Along with the Mussolini bust (which had also been displayed at the *Second Biennial Roman International Exposition*, while another copy belonged to Mussolini), McCormack exhibited busts of Ezra Pound, the Italian archaeologist Giacomo Boni, and Lidia Rismondo, the widow of a war hero. See F. D., "Two Brilliant Artists Show in Paris Mansion," *Paris—Evening Telegraph*, March 28, 1924. Edgar and Elsie Palmer Payne Papers, DeRu's Fine Arts, Bellflower, CA.

62. The elder Seligmann had assisted Benjamin Altman in building his collection of important old master paintings, which was left to the Metropolitan Museum of Art in 1913. "J. Seligmann Dies: Noted Art Dealer," *New York Times*, November 1, 1923. John Russell, "Germain Seligman, Dealer and Expert in French Art," *New York Times*, March 28, 1978. Germain Seligman (1893–1978) dropped the second *n* in his name at some point after his father's death. The catalogue for Payne's exhibition lists the gallery as Galeries Jacques Seligmann, Germain Seligmann & Cie., Successeurs. The New York gallery, Jacques Seligmann & Co., was located at 705 Fifth Avenue.

63. H. S. C., "Paris," *Art News* 22 (April 12, 1924): 9.

64. F. D., "Two Brilliant Artists."

65. The works on view were *La Sierra Nevada—Californie, Barque de Pêche, Eaux Vénitiennes, Neiges Éternelles—Mont Blanc, Versant du Wetterhorn, Paysage—Grindelwald, Grandeur des Alpes—La Jungfrau, Spiez-sur-Lac, Sentinelle* (known today as *Sentinels of the Coast, Monterey*), *L'Hiver, Le Glacier Haut, Voiles au Soleil, Sommets Neigeux, Haut Sommet*, and *Paysage Montagneux*.

66. "Les expositions particulières: Mme Nancy Cox McCormack et M. Edgar Alwin Payne à Hôtel Seligmann," *La revue moderne illustrée des arts et de la vie*, May 15, 1924. Edgar and Elsie Palmer Payne Papers, DeRu's Fine Arts, Bellflower, CA.

67. Payne, *Composition of Outdoor Painting*, 64.

68. "Expositions particulières," *Revue moderne*.

69. H. S. C., "Paris."

70. "Two Well-Known American Artists Exhibit Bronzes and Paintings," *New York Herald*, Paris ed., March 16, 1924. Edgar and Elsie Palmer Payne Papers, DeRu's Fine Arts, Bellflower, CA.

71. F. D., "Two Brilliant Artists."

72. Given that this work was illustrated in the *Chicago Evening Post* in December with a caption indicating it had been shown at the Paris Salon of 1924, it appears that *Les Hauteurs* was also known as *Snow-Clad Heights*. Its composition is similar to another Wellhorn scene, *Sunlit Peak*, included in Payne's 1926 Stendahl Galleries show. "'Snow-Clad Heights'—Edgar Alwin Payne," *Chicago Evening Post*, December 16, 1924. Edgar and Elsie Palmer Payne Papers, DeRu's Fine Arts, Bellflower, CA.

73. Undated article from *The Latin Quarter*.

74. "Paris Salon Stirs Trouble with Artists: Groups Foreign Exhibitors by Themselves—Frenchmen Join in Protest," *New York Times*, April 30, 1924.

75. Simon Arbellot, "Un petit incident aux artistes français," *Le Figaro* (Paris), May 3, 1924. Edgar and Elsie Palmer Payne Papers, DeRu's Fine Arts, Bellflower, CA. For Czedekowski's painting, see http://www.delvaux.auction.fr/UK/vente_peintures_arts_graphiques/v10170_delvaux/l1466135_boleslas_jan_czedekowski_1885_1969_portrait_homme_1924_.html, accessed January 16, 2010.

76. Anderson and Hogue, *Payne and His Work*, 18 (no. 1).

77. These included château de Loches, which was designed and occupied by Henry II of England and his son Richard the Lionheart during the twelfth century, exhibited at the Stendahl Galleries in 1927; château de Josselin, in southern Brittany on the river Oust, illustrated in Coen, *Paynes, Edgar & Elsie*, 43; and château de Combourg, in northern Brittany near Saint-Malo, illustrated in "Edgar

Alwin Payne Has New Showing in Galleries," *Allerton House Magazine,* May 1929, 6. Edgar and Elsie Palmer Payne Papers, DeRu's Fine Arts, Bellflower, CA.

78. Evelyn further observed that the "women still wore the traditional clothes and the coif on their heads that were different for each area" and that "wooden shoes were worn by all." Hatcher, *Drawings of Edgar Payne,* 48.

79. Elsie Palmer Payne, quoted in Marquis, "Southland Artist."

80. Another model is illustrated in Hatcher, *Drawings of Edgar Payne,* 47.

81. The German-built SS *Leviathan* had been a troop ship for the Allies in World War I. Its reconditioning was completed in June 1923.

82. This exhibition was held from January 30 to March 10, 1925.

83. Anderson, Of Art and Artists, March 29, 1925. Anderson erroneously identified the gallery as Newcastle-Macklin. Edgar and Elsie Palmer Payne Papers, DeRu's Fine Arts, Bellflower, CA.

84. Caroline Walker, "Art Exhibition Vivifies Cal. Mountains," newspaper clipping, 1926, Edgar and Elsie Palmer Payne Papers, DeRu's Fine Arts, Bellflower, CA. This painting is probably the same as *Boats of Cameret* [*sic*], illustrated in Anderson and Hogue, *Payne and His Work,* 30 (no. 13). *Peaks and Shadows* is also illustrated in the aforementioned book, 45 (no. 28).

85. [Antony Anderson], "Some Newsy Notes on Matters of Art," *Los Angeles Times,* May 31, 1925. Edgar and Elsie Palmer Payne Papers, DeRu's Fine Arts, Bellflower, CA.

86. Marquis, "Southland Artist."

87. "Edgar Payne's Paintings," *Chicago Evening Post,* November 10, 1925. Edgar and Elsie Palmer Payne Papers, DeRu's Fine Arts, Bellflower, CA.

88. Hogue, "Art of Edgar Payne."

89. Arthur Millier, "From Alpine Peaks to Restful Harbors," *Los Angeles Times,* May 23, 1926. Edgar and Elsie Palmer Payne Papers, DeRu's Fine Arts, Bellflower, CA.

90. "Colorful Vessels . . . and Alpine Crags," newspaper clipping, 1926, Edgar and Elsie Palmer Payne Papers, DeRu's Fine Arts, Bellflower, CA; Hogue, "Art of Edgar Payne"; Walker, "Art Exhibition."

91. This was a pre-Revolutionary house to which a studio had been added.

92. This exhibition was held in April 1927. See Coen, *Paynes, Edgar & Elsie,* 95.

93. Sonia Wolfson, "Art and Artists: Payne and Gilbert at Stendahl's," *California Graphic,* May 28, 1927. Edgar and Elsie Palmer Payne Papers, DeRu's Fine Arts, Bellflower, CA.

94. Hogue, "God of the Mountains."

95. "Stuber and Payne," *Los Angeles Times,* January 22, 1928. Edgar and Elsie Palmer Payne Papers, DeRu's Fine Arts, Bellflower, CA.

96. "Gossip from Studios," *Los Angeles Times,* August 19, 1928. Edgar and Elsie Palmer Payne Papers, DeRu's Fine Arts, Bellflower, CA.

97. The departure of the *Minnekahda* on June 9, 1928, was reported in "14 Liners to Sail for Foreign Ports," *New York Times,* June 9, 1928. The ship departed from New York and made stops in Plymouth, England; Boulogne, France; and London before returning across the Atlantic.

98. Coen, *Paynes, Edgar & Elsie,* 54.

99. The registration listed his address as 8, boulevard Caracael, Nice. Permis de circulation, no. 31/2, Préfet du département d'Alpes Maritimes, July 24, 1928. Registration for a Model T Ford. Edgar and Elsie Palmer Payne Papers, DeRu's Fine Arts, Bellflower, CA.

100. George Brandriff file, Laguna Art Museum, Archives.

101. Passenger Lists of Vessels Arriving at New York, New York, 1820–1897 (National Archives Microfilm Publication M237, 675 rolls); Records of the US Customs Service, Record Group 36; National Archives, Washington, DC. Source Citation: Year: *1928;* Microfilm Serial: *T715;* Microfilm Roll: *T715_4349;* Line: *27;* Page Number: *30.* Source Information: www.ancestry.com, *New York Passenger Lists, 1820–1957* (online database). Provo, UT: Ancestry.com Operations, Inc., 2010.

102. Payne, *Composition of Outdoor Painting,* vii.

EDGAR PAYNE'S
SOUTHWEST

Peter H. Hassrick

Director Emeritus
Petrie Institute of Western American Art,
Denver Art Museum

In the January 1929 issue of *Touring Topics,* the official voice of the Automobile Club of Southern California of Los Angeles, the magazine's editors offered a brief but affectionate critique of their hometown celebrity landscape painter, William Wendt. They applauded his sedentary disposition with the observation that "some of the friends of his youth have wandered about the earth, grown more famous, sold more paintings. Wendt, once California had conquered him, stayed and fought out his battle alone." Wendt had by that date spent twenty-two years as a resident of Los Angeles. So completely and exclusively had he absorbed the countryside of the region, the editors felt it would have been "impossible to imagine Wendt apart from this great land of southern California."[1]

Six months later, in the *South Coast News* of Laguna Beach, art critic Antony Anderson wrote about Wendt's friend, fellow artist, and Los Angeles neighbor Edgar Payne. The headline, "Edgar Payne, Painter and World Traveler," suggested a rather different personality. Reviewing an exhibition of twenty-six Payne canvases at the Biltmore Salon in Los Angeles, Anderson defined an artistic personality that was in fact the antithesis of Wendt's. "Yesterday in France, today in California, tomorrow in Canada among the Rockies—that's Payne's life, and he travels with plenty of fresh paints and clean brushes in hand." Payne,

according to Anderson, led "the ideal life for a landscape painter." He was peripatetic, he was adventuresome, and "he always traveled with his wife and daughter in a high powered car."[2]

Wendt and Payne, aside from the apparent differences in the pace and breadth of their lives, shared much in common. They had both come of age artistically in Chicago. They were both essentially self-trained, with only brief exposure to formal instruction at the Art Institute of Chicago. And they had both settled in Southern California while maintaining enduring connections with their Chicago roots. As landscape painters, they had developed similarly as well, moving through a period of modified Impressionism to a style that replaced velvety, tonal color harmonies in nature with vigorous, broadly brushed works—poetry supplanted by grandeur. What Anderson said of Payne's paintings in 1929 could also have applied to Wendt's of the same period: "Payne sees nature in a big and comprehensive way, and something of this bigness of outlook he communicates to us."[3]

Yet, by degrees, Payne took his bigness to another level. It was a function of his adventuresome personality. No horizon was too far for him; no vista, regardless of how daunting, was too intimidating. Wendt famously remarked in 1924 that he refused to paint the Grand Canyon because it was simply impossible.[4] Payne could not fathom the impossible. He had

P. 176: *Red Mesa, Monument Valley, Utah* (detail, p. 212), c. 1935

Opposite: *South Rim, Grand Canyon* (detail, p. 198), after 1929

EDGAR PAYNE

already been to the Grand Canyon at least once by 1929 and was preparing for a second trip the next year . . . that is, as soon as he had digested and interpreted the awesome grandeur of the Canadian Rockies, which would welcome the artist, his family, and their "high powered car" into their embrace that summer.

In a biographical sketch written after Payne's death by his widow and fellow artist, Elsie Palmer Payne, it is suggested that of all the locations that beckoned him as a muse, the American Southwest was perhaps the most compelling. The Paynes were still in Chicago when they embarked on their first extended summer trip to Arizona and New Mexico:[5] "In 1916 the Santa Fe Railroad, just opening that country to tourists, sent him . . . to paint the Indian Pueblos and Mesas and mountains of New Mexico and the Canyon de Chelley [sic], Monument Valley and Grand Canyon of Arizona." Elsie went on to say that "he returned to that glorious country nearly every year that he was in America the rest of his life. It was the last place he painted before his final illness."[6]

Payne's romance with the Southwest began, in part at least, vicariously through the works of artists with whom he exhibited in Chicago in 1911. He and William Wendt presented California mountain vistas at the Art Institute of Chicago that year. These were hung alongside Edward Potthast's *Deepening Shadows* (a view of the Grand Canyon) and Albert Groll's etching *Superstition Mountain—Arizona*.[7] Payne first visited California in 1909, and his train had passed through the heart of Arizona and New Mexico, so he had seen some of the territory firsthand. The Atchison, Topeka & Santa Fe Railway, which Payne would have ridden west, had been promoting the Grand Canyon as a destination for travelers since the early 1900s.[8]

Monument Valley, Riverbed, after 1929. Oil on canvas, 25¼ x 30¼ in. Private collection. Courtesy of The Irvine Museum

Potthast had been the railway company's guest, along with four other prominent landscape artists, on a special all-expenses-paid trip to the canyon in 1910.[9]

Over the next several years, moving back and forth from what was known as his favorite sketching ground, California, and his Chicago studio, Payne established a method and a vision that would serve him well into the future. In California he made studies of the remarkable hills, coastline, and mountains. But his sketches were just the beginning. "Works of art must be more than that: they must also express one's ideal," he told a reporter in 1914. And his ideal could be achieved only at home. "So Mr. Payne paints all his exhibition pictures in his studio in Chicago."[10]

The appeal of his work went well beyond Chicago. When the Peoria Society of Allied Arts purchased an impressive oil titled *The Hills of Marin* in 1914, Payne revealed an additional dimension of his artistic vision. When asked what he was trying to express, he replied, "To show the bigness of the hills and the beauty of the passing clouds."[11] California had opened up for him, according to one critic, "a new world of air and sunshine" that allowed him to develop "the striking qualities of light and color he now possesses."[12] So combined, his attraction to grand scale, or "bigness," and his devotion to "beauty," or what color and light can do to visually enhance mass, exposed his artistic strategy. His works were inspired by nature but "humanized in the studio."[13]

A substantial part of Payne's studio time during the first decade of the twentieth century was devoted to another aspect of his artistic life—the production of murals. He could exhibit, and from time to time sell, his landscapes, which helped him support a new family (his daughter, Evelyn, was born early in

1914), but murals were his bread and butter. Of particular note at this time was his set of murals for the American Theater in Chicago. Twenty-one large canvases composed his commission, which called for a series of historical tableaux from America's past. One of these, referred to as a twenty-six-foot panel depicting "a prairie schooner train of the forty-niners in the West," might have profited from his travels to and from California. A Chicago newspaper opined that Payne's murals were "far ahead of what is generally expected in the adornment of theaters,"[14] but the figures were wooden, the backgrounds were uninspired, and there is no evidence that views from his western sojourns had any specific role in the development of these murals.

One of Payne's patrons at this time was Chicago's mayor and leading art impresario, Carter H. Harrison Jr. At the joint exhibition of Payne and Nancy Cox-McCormack presented at Chicago's Palette & Chisel Club, the artist sold Harrison two Ventura County landscapes. It was an event worthy of mention in the *Chicago Daily Tribune*.[15] Harrison was a major champion of New Mexico, especially the dusty village of Taos, as a subject for artists. That fall, he and a group of like-minded patrons would underwrite expenses for Payne's friend Walter Ufer, a fellow member of the Palette & Chisel Club, to go to Taos. Ufer, a figure painter, was immediately enchanted by Indian and Hispanic life in New Mexico, while Payne's devotion was to landscape work. Harrison preferred the former genre, and Payne was not offered a similar deal. Two years later, when Harrison attended an exhibition of works by Payne and figure painter E. Martin Hennings at the Art Institute of Chicago, it was again a figure painter who came under Harrison's wing and got a free ride to Taos. Payne would have to search elsewhere for such support.

The West and Southwest, as distinct from California, reckoned large among Chicago's artists in the middle of the decade. At the favorite center for activities among many of the Chicago artist corps, the Palette & Chisel Club, there was a constant buzz about the West as a promising subject for creative work. Club members enthusiastically organized a special "western night" in 1915 when celebrated cowboy artist Charles Russell visited the city.[16] That same year, the Paynes and others brought back tales of wonder after visiting the Panama-Pacific International Exposition in San Francisco. There the Fred Harvey Company, in concert with the Santa Fe Railway, constructed a six-acre replica exhibit of the Grand Canyon to compete with Union Pacific's reproduction of Yellowstone's Old Faithful. The exposition's art exhibits drew much attention as well, and not just because of their modernist displays. The famous critic, collector, and curator Christian Brinton proclaimed, "The West has a great future in art. Indeed, I go so far as to say the future of art belongs to the West."[17] Late that summer, Walter Ufer returned to Chicago from New Mexico and the Grand Canyon. By November, his paintings were reported to "have brought him many thousands of dollars."[18] Although none of the six founding members of the Taos Society of Artists came from Chicago, the group held one of its first exhibitions there in 1915, at the department store Carson Pirie Scott. It was, according to founding member Ernest Blumenschein, the society's big start.[19] Chicago was very responsive. Three of the hometown artists—Walter Ufer, Victor Higgins, and E. Martin Hennings (all close friends of Payne)—were soon officially accepted into the society.

So when, in the summer of 1916, Payne decided to take his palette and brushes, his family, and his peripatetic disposition into the Southwest, why did he *not* choose Taos? Walter Ufer commented to the press that year that Taos was welcoming, available, and essentially untouched. "It is the variety, the depth and the breadth of it, rooted in eons of time . . . which explain the secret of its infinite charm. The portrait painter, the landscape artist, the limner of character, the genre and historical painter, every school and every temperament, will here find their heart desires."[20] Yet Payne was known for his determined independence and his search for remote locations. And while Taos was certainly not on any main line, it was already, by 1916, almost overly popular. Blumenschein wrote that in the summers around this time, more than a hundred artists would visit Taos, a perfect reason for Payne to divert his attentions elsewhere.[21]

In addition, Payne had clearly expressed himself about his vision as an artist, and it did not include expending effort on the mundane. The Pueblo Indians were a pastoral, agrarian people who by mid-decade had become *the* most popular indigenous culture in America.[22] The Pueblo were picturesque, but the Navajo, with their nomadic ways and their expansive geographic realm, were considered sublime.[23] Payne responded to "bigness," and Navajo land promised all that he could imagine.

With war in Europe, the widely read New York art critic Henry McBride encouraged artists to explore new American haunts and to experiment, "make voyages of discovery." He applauded New York painters E. Irving Couse and Ernest Blumenschein for venturing into the "untrammeled" "far corner of northwest

Canyon Riders, n.d. Oil on canvas, 25 x 30 in. Collection of Reed and Chris Halladay

New Mexico" and Edward Potthast for ranging even farther, to the rim of the Grand Canyon.[24]

But the major factor regarding Payne's selection of Navajo land rather than the Rio Grande pueblos probably came down to patronage. The Santa Fe Railway was vigorously attempting to promote its Chicago–Los Angeles line. A new train it called "The Navajo" had just been put into service in 1915, and the promotions department was anxious to increase ridership. In addition, the railroad had invested vast amounts of money in developing accommodations and amenities around the Grand Canyon. Landscape painters were in demand, and someone with Payne's freshness of vision and adventuresome spirit would be a welcome addition to the scene.

In the spring of 1916, Ufer and Payne exhibited together in Peoria. Ufer showed his studies of "Indian life" from Taos, while Payne's California views, glimmering with light, captured "the western mountains, gigantic, yet softly aerial."[25] Ufer went off that summer to his beloved Taos, again under the sponsorship of Carter Harrison. The year before, he had, under the aegis of William H. Simpson, general advertising agent for the Santa Fe Railway, visited the Grand Canyon. Upon his return, he sold Simpson his oil *Grand Canyon from El Tovar* (Santa Fe Railway Collection, Fort Worth, Texas) for the railroad's corporate collection. He may have connected Payne with Simpson for a similar arrangement. Payne had to put up as collateral one of his California landscapes, and by mid-June the artist had letters of introduction to C. A. Brant, manager of the El Tovar Hotel at the Grand Canyon, and Roman Hubbell of Gallup, New Mexico, a well-established trader among the Navajo.[26] Simpson told Brant that Payne was "an

artist of considerable note in the East" and offered to compensate the hotel $100 for the artist's expenses. Simpson offered Payne an additional $100 for other expenses related to securing sketches for a painting of Canyon de Chelly and a pledge of $200 more once the final painting was completed and accepted for the railroad's collection. Simpson provided train fare for the artist and his family and arranged with Hubbell to cover all costs of the family's transportation to and from Canyon de Chelly.

Roman Hubbell wrote to Simpson from Gallup on June 25 that "Mr. Edgar Payne, wife and baby arrived here in 'good condition' and we sent them out in a special car to Canyon de Chelly this morning. Every courtesy in our power will be extended them while on this trip."[27] It is not known how long Payne and family had planned to stay in the Canyon de Chelly area, but it was a distinct surprise to Brant at the Grand Canyon when almost five months later, on October 15, they finally appeared on the threshold of the El Tovar Hotel. Not only that, but, as Brant wrote to Simpson, Payne announced that he was going to stay at the canyon only a few days and wanted to use the balance of the $100 allotted for his canyon visit to buy "Navajo blankets and curios." The Grand Canyon, though extraordinarily magnificent, had been painted by scores of artists before, including his friend Ufer, and appears not to have particularly interested Payne at this time. Simpson, who is typically portrayed as inflexible, eventually, though reluctantly, consented to Payne's unusual expenditure request. He must have been pleased with the results of Payne's labors among the Navajos.

By March 1917, Payne had supplied Simpson with no fewer than eleven paintings of Canyon de Chelly

EDGAR PAYNE

country from which to choose. The railway accepted one of the paintings, *Sunset, Canyon de Chelly* (opposite), in exchange for the California landscape plus $200. The painting, according to Simpson, was "thoroughly appreciated" by him and his assistant, C. J. Birchfield. Another oil, *Navajo Country* (whereabouts unknown), was acquired for $250.[28] Both were shipped to Detroit, eventually to decorate the offices of the railway's Michigan headquarters. *Navajo Country* was later sent to Gallup for the opening of Fred Harvey's new El Navajo Hotel in the spring of 1918. It is thought to have remained there at least through the first phase of the hotel's existence, until 1923.

Sunset, Canyon de Chelly, while moderate in scale as a canvas, is immense in its rendition of nature's architectonic grandeur. The canyon, the historical stronghold of the Navajo people, is presented as a colossal fortress on the one hand and as a glowing spiritual sanctuary on the other. The Navajo people, dwarfed on the canyon floor by the overarching monoliths of red sandstone, add both scale and quietude to the scene. They ride away from the viewer and into the light as if leading the viewer into a realm beyond comprehension, one entered only by the most intrepid. The partial insertion of dappled blue sky suggests that there is in this domain only limited accommodation for a celestial presence.

Another surviving painting of this period, *Canyon de Chelly* (p. 192), renders the same mood. Unlike the sunset picture, however, which exudes a cool elegance, *Canyon de Chelly* is staged in midday. The distant escarpment, fully illuminated by the sun, presents a palpable tension between the full force of Arizona's summer heat and the shadowed relief

Sunset, Canyon de Chelly, 1916. Oil on canvas, 28 x 34 in. Mark C. Pigott Collection

Canyon de Chelly, n.d. Oil on canvas, 28 x 34 in. Private collection

in which the riders seek refuge. *Canyon de Chelly* was purchased by or given to the Hubbell family as a memento of Payne's long stay in the area.

In these two works, nature's architecture predominates. Other artists were coming to similar conclusions about indigenous human construction in the Southwest. Victor Higgins commented to a Chicago reporter, for example, that the Pueblo buildings were "the only naturally American architecture in the nation today."[29] The walls of Canyon de Chelly and Canyon del Muerto were, for Payne, an even more purely American yet natural form of architecture. The Navajo had been dwelling within them for more than a century.

Payne's friend and compatriot Carl Oscar Borg was in the canyon that same summer, and the two

men may have worked together. Borg also produced a view from the canyon floor titled *Sunset, Canyon de Chelly,* which was sold to Simpson that year (below left). It has been called Borg's masterpiece.[30]

Although such scenes were novel for Simpson, views of Navajo people surrendered to the enormity of their natural home were not new. Photographer Edward S. Curtis had recorded similarly juxtaposed elements in his 1904 print *Cañon de Chelly—Navajo* (p. 191). One of Payne's on-site studies, an oil sketch that is perhaps from this period (p. 190), pictures a graceful stone hip that holds in place the unseen walls above. He made a stunning charcoal study of the scene as well (p. 190). Here, as with Curtis, he was willing to reveal the sky as part of the composition.

Above left: Carl Oscar Borg (American, b. Sweden, 1879–1947). *Sunset, Canyon de Chelly,* 1916. Oil on canvas, 40 x 30 in. Santa Fe Collection of Southwestern Art. Reprinted with permission of the BNSF Railway

Above right: *Edgar Payne in His Studio Painting Canyon de Chelly,* n.d. Photographer unknown

Left: *Light and Shadowed Cliffs, Canyon de Chelly*, c. 1930. Oil on canvas, 11 x 14 in. Courtesy of DeRu's Fine Arts

Below: *Canyon de Chelly*, after 1929. Charcoal on paper, 16 x 18 in. Collection of Martin and Brigitte Medak

Payne entered at least two of his southwestern works in the annual exhibition of the Art Institute of Chicago in 1917—one titled *Navajo Country* (later purchased by Simpson) and the other *A Navajo Pastoral*. The whereabouts of these two oils is unknown today, but they probably resembled a canvas pictured in a photograph of Payne in his studio with Evelyn (p. 193). This is the antithesis of his canyon pictures. The Indians, now proportionately more substantial in scale, ride above the horizon line. They are liberated from the sandstone chasm and silhouetted against an animated, cloudy, Baroque sky. He was developing a formula that would be reapplied a dozen years later and employed successfully from the 1930s into the 1940s.

Although Payne was searching for solitude among the Navajo in the summer of 1916, he was definitely not alone. Several other artists, like Borg retreating from the normal artist haunts as McBride had suggested, found their way into Navajo land. New York painter William R. Leigh stayed much of the summer with John Lorenzo Hubbell, Roman's father, near Ganado, Arizona. He painted Canyon de Chelly but focused primarily on the Navajo people and their

Edward S. Curtis (American, 1868–1952). *Cañon de Chelly—Navajo*, 1904. Platinum print photograph, 18 x 22 in. Denver Public Library, Western History Collection

Canyon de Chelly, 1916. Oil on canvas, 27½ x 33¼ in. Courtesy of the National Park Service, Hubbell Trading Post National Historic Site, HUTR 5279

ubiquitous flocks of goats and sheep. Payne disregarded this vital source of Navajo life despite the fact that the region had literally become overrun by sheep by 1916, and approximately seventy-five trading posts like Hubbell's routinely bought and traded wool.[31]

Critics in New York passed off Leigh's large narrative canvases, such as *Land of His Fathers* (location unknown), as fatuous, romantic illustrations, but they admired one, a small oil titled *The Sentinel* (p. 195), as a real work of art, praising its lack of pretentiousness and its tonal harmonies, tenderness, and suggestion of human feeling.[32] This, and a shared sense of loss and an elegiac mood, ally Leigh's *The Sentinel* with the unknown painting by Payne that appears in the 1916 photograph of the artist and his daughter (below right).

Ufer and Hennings, at the request of Harrison, focused on the living Pueblo people. In their paintings the Indians worked with horses, labored in the cornfield, and basically fulfilled the requirements of everyday life. The artists rarely succumbed to allegorical treatments or historicizing, unlike their Taos compatriots Bert Geer Phillips and E. Irving Couse, so their work enjoys a certain freshness. Payne found his niche situating the Navajo somewhere in between these two interpretations. Nowhere, for example, did he retreat into the old days of the Navajo; rather, he kept his images of them as current as the day he first sketched or photographed them. And yet, unlike Ufer and Hennings, Payne employed Indians in his paintings primarily as decorative motifs. They performed no quotidian tasks and provided no hint of their human functions in life other than demonstrating their skills in horsemanship. They were primarily compositional devices, employed in groups to center a composition or, at times, offset to one side to counterbalance a

vast expanse or a prominent geologic feature. One of the most ubiquitous features of Canyon de Chelly has long been the rock art and elegant ruins of the pre-Navajo culture, the Anasazi. Payne seemed to be as oblivious to these elements as he was to the sheep. Yet he was not alone in his disregard. Borg, along with Maynard Dixon and Buck Weaver, all artist friends of Payne who walked and rode through the canyon with their sketchbooks and paints that summer, generally avoided reference to those fascinating prehistoric vestiges in their finished work.

Payne's prolonged visit to New Mexico and Arizona in 1916 appears to have produced a rather limited body of work and seems to have been a singular event in his early career. Despite Elsie's earlier quoted contention that "he returned to that glorious country nearly every year that he was in America the rest of his life," there is no evidence either in his

Edgar Payne and His Daughter, Evelyn, in the Studio, c. 1916. Photographer unknown. Courtesy of DeRu's Fine Arts

Navajo Country, n.d. Oil on canvas, 32 x 40 in. Collection of Paul and Kathleen Bagley

subsequent art production or in itineraries of his travels to substantiate that claim.[33] After 1917 he stopped exhibiting works related to the area, which would imply that he had ceased visiting the Navajo and had refrained from painting them and their homeland as well. Given Payne's belief that fresh observation resulted in the most compelling studio production, he was no doubt loath to return to southwestern themes without renewed visitation.

Payne's known exhibition records until 1931 contain no southwestern paintings. His major one-man show at the Stendahl Galleries of Los Angeles in 1926 comprised over sixty works. Not one derived from the Southwest, and one reviewer, Mary Marsh for the *Los Angeles Times,* in fact complained about his limit of focus—a concentration on his recent trips to Europe and the High Sierra. "It seems to be his nature to concentrate upon one or two motives," she wrote, and his "limitation of theme and repetition of method" resulted in a "lack of variety in the exhibition."[34] Another reporter observed that in 1926 it was "among the great peaks of the Alps and the high Sierras that Payne has found his spiritual home. I have a feeling that he will return again and again to them."[35]

It was not until 1927 and a commission to provide eight murals for the new Hotel St. Paul in Los Angeles that Payne drew once again on his Southwest experience. One of the murals, *The Covered Wagon* (p. 196), suggests a spiritual return to the vast desert and canyon land he had experienced in 1916. The murals are lost today, but this one, at least, may have given Payne cause to reconsider a forgotten theme. Certainly, compared with his earlier American Theater mural of a similar subject, the Los Angeles mural is more site specific.

Within a couple of years, Payne began to spread his wings again and reopen his horizons. In 1929 he, his wife and daughter, and their high-powered car headed for the Canadian Rockies. This trip, along with what was viewed as an unusually fine showing of southwestern paintings at the Stendahl Galleries by Payne's confreres Nicolai Fechin, Walter Ufer, Frank Tenney Johnson, Armin Hansen, and James Swinnerton, may have reawakened his interest in the American heartland.[36] Critics seemed to come alive

William R. Leigh (American, 1866–1955). *The Sentinel,* 1917. Oil on canvas, 17½ x 16 in. Denver Art Museum, Bernadette Berger Collection. Image courtesy of the Denver Art Museum

to his new themes as well, especially when he presented his freshly painted Canadian mountain scenes at Chicago's Illinois Women's Athletic Club. Critic Eleanor Jewett of the *Chicago Daily Tribune* termed the show a "brilliant exhibition" and commended the artist for the span of his vision and for bringing a breath of Canadian inspiration to Chicago.[37]

What exactly prompted Payne's return to the Southwest in 1930 is not known. Maybe he found motivation in reading about the Santa Fe Railway and Fred Harvey Company's Indian-Detours, which opened up the Navajo country that year to car tours of the canyons and Monument Valley (opposite). Perhaps he read in the Automobile Club of Southern California's magazine, *Touring Topics,* his friend Borg's account of "the province of Tusayan," the land of the Hopi and the Navajo. "In its varying moods this country seems endless," wrote Borg. "There is no end to the light, color, form and distances."[38] Such a place could rejuvenate Payne and help him circumvent Mary Marsh's

criticisms of a limited scope to his work. For whatever reason, he seems to have once again been hooked.

In the spring of 1934 Payne wrote to C. J. Birchfield, who had become general advertising agent for the Santa Fe Railway after Simpson passed away the year before. In his letter, Payne, while soliciting another free ride to the Southwest, mentioned that he had "been sketching . . . through the Canyon de Chelly country . . . and also around Gallup for the last three years." He also hoped to go again that August and would "probably do some work around the Grand Canyon" as well (p. 198).[39] He sought a rendezvous with Birchfield, but unfortunately neither a commission nor a get-together ever happened. The letter does reveal, though, that once he had returned to "Indian country," as Birchfield referred to it, Payne had established a sustained pattern.

By the time Payne revisited the Southwest, his style had changed substantially. Since he rarely dated his works, it is difficult to distinguish stylistically

The Covered Wagon, 1927. Oil on canvas, dimensions unknown. From a photograph of a mural in the Hotel St. Paul, Los Angeles. Image courtesy of the archives of the Laguna Art Museum

his paintings of the 1930s from those of the early 1940s. Yet compared with his works of 1916, these new oils were far bolder in execution, more adventuresome in composition, and more expansive in palette. Moreover, in 1930 he entered Navajo land from the north, coming from Ogden, Utah, through Monument Valley, so even the topography was different from what he had seen in 1916.

The *Salt Lake Tribune* reported on Payne's stay in Utah in July 1930 and critiqued an exhibition of his works at the Hotel Utah in Salt Lake City. The article called Payne the "poet painter of the High Sierras," one especially able to imbue his canvases with "a deep lyric quality."[40] And now, it said, he was poised to embark on a journey to "the Arizona desert via our southern wonderland, where he plans to secure a picture or two."[41]

Subsequent exhibitions in 1931, in New York at the National Academy of Design and in Chicago at the city's mecca for businessmen, the Midland Club, reveal a substantial production of major southwestern works following his initial return to the region, not just one or two pictures. The Midland Club display contained thirty-four canvases, approximately one-third of which had been inspired by Payne's Southwest travels. About half of those were landscapes; the rest were scenes of Navajo riders.[42] They contributed to what was regarded as a "stunning show."[43]

Over the next fifteen years, the Southwest consistently engaged Payne's imagination. When he motored through Monument Valley over those years, he persistently reapplied his early mantra about the seminal importance of "bigness" of mountain mass and the "beauty" of clouds. Now energized with the force of his expressionist brushwork and a heightened palette, he embraced the atmospheric clarity of the subject

and was able to create such masterworks as *Red Mesa, Monument Valley, Utah* (p. 212). In time he would produce multiple views of the same scene from different vantage points and with equally thrilling cloud effects. He patiently sought the best time of day so he could render Monument Valley's spectacular features in glowing iridescence, as seen in *Monument Valley* (p. 213).

Often Payne incorporated Navajo riders into his mesa landscapes. His painting *Burning the Hogan* (p. 206) was created for the Leon McSparron family, who operated the Thunderbird Ranch near Canyon de Chelly.[44] In it Payne offered an unusual narrative component. A gentle reminder of a perceived passing culture, the oil portrays three riders looking back

Unknown artist. *Indian–detours*, 1930. Brochure cover, 8 x 9 in. Courtesy of University of Arizona Libraries, Special Collections

South Rim, Grand Canyon, after 1929. Oil on canvas, 25 x 30 in. J. Dutra Collection

over their shoulders at a twilight horizon. A column of smoke rises from the base of a rock escarpment as a hogan burns in the distance. The Navajo had a custom that when a man died in his hogan, he would be cremated there by his family and friends. For Payne, this was no rhetorical gesture; it was heartfelt reverie that deserved what was, for him, a rare narrative portrayal.

Compositions like this and variations on the theme such as *Navajo Country* (p. 207)—a painting he created in 1942 for his close friends Lloyd and Janet Ambrose of Thoreau, New Mexico, with whom he generally stayed—were carefully formatted before being painted. They derived from figural studies (p. 200) of what he called at the time a modified "steelyard" composition, which was in his mind "probably the most popular and possibly the simplest form of balance in general use."[45] This structural device provided a powerful graphic armature onto which to construct his picture. But beyond that, it was his choice to cast the riders in shadow and to have them look back on a sunny horizon, and it was that choice that provided the stirring metaphor of human loss and passing that conveys the heart of Payne's sentiment.

Payne alternated these paintings of cultural evanescence with sunnier treatments that inverted the perception of Navajo passing. Works such as *Untitled [Clouds and Riders]* (p. 208) engage the horsemen in a halcyon moment wherein a carefree sky invites ebullient thoughts of cheer. Even when rain sheets down through the distant sky, as in *Two Indians in Southwest Landscape* (p. 209), there is a sense that the air is laden with joy and levity provided by the rich perfume of welcome moisture.

Payne made a practice of photographing Navajo people when he visited Arizona and New Mexico after 1930. Some of these prints survive (p. 201) and were no doubt used, along with large-scale figural drawings (p. 200), to help format and breathe life into canvases such as *Navajos* (p. 204) and *Navajo Riders* (p. 205), paintings in which the Indians dominate the landscape and serve as exotic interlocutors into a world of wonder and beauty.

Ultimately, the titan masses of Canyon de Chelly's enchanting cliffs drew Payne to their embrace in these late years. As he returned to them time after time, he sought to reveal their power not so much, as earlier, through their enveloping omnipresence but with recognition of their ability to capture and refract light. *Blue Canyon* (p. 210), a view from the south rim, is the perfect combination of sunshine, light, and shadow defining the majesty of the precipice below. Fresh in its perspective and inviting in its teasing openness, this vista exemplifies Payne's mature artistic strategy.

Even in scenes of the canyon floor, such as *Navajo Stronghold* (p. 211) and *Canyon de Chelly* (pp. 216–217), it is the sun's play on the faceted, varnish-streaked abutments that commands attention. Payne's vital, broad brushstrokes mirror the textured facade, but it is his rendering of light that brings the scenes to life. He returns to his affection for architectonic form. His reality and vision mirror that of his fellow Chicago painter Victor Higgins, who in 1932 famously wrote about the architectural basis for art and its connection to the modernism in art:

> The modern painter, and by "modern" I do not mean exactly the painter who is a distortionist or an innovator, but a true

Left: *Study for Western Painting,* c. 1929.
Pencil on paper, 16 x 20 in. Image courtesy
of Scottsdale Art Auction

Below: *Composition Study for Navajo Horsemen,*
after 1929. Pencil on paper, 12 x 17 in.
Collection of Ruth and Robert Mirvis

Right: *Three Navajo Riders,* c. 1930.
Photograph by Edgar Payne. Courtesy of
DeRu's Fine Arts

modern, builds his picture, he does not merely paint it. He has his superstructure, his foundation, just as an architect has his buildings. These must be true mathematically or his picture is going to fall down on him. Very few laymen understand this underlying science of art and it is a pity. I wish they might learn.[46]

In these late southwestern paintings, Payne manifested an artist's true affection for his subject. As the forms and light disclosed nature's rhythms and made their way to the surface of his canvases, he incorporated their cadence and meter into his vision of what art should mean. Most art forms—dance, poetry, and music, for example—must be governed by rhythm, he wrote. So too must painting. And when nature's countenance and the artist's disposition were in harmony, great art could result. Just as some creative talents could orchestrate euphonious chords for the ear, Payne used his virtuosity to work visual miracles meant to expose what he called the "spiritual flow which encircles animate and inanimate nature—the rhythm of life and the universe."[47]

Navajo Riders on Horseback, after 1929. Oil on canvas, 28 x 34 in. Collection of Reed and Chris Halladay

EDGAR PAYNE

Navajos, after 1929. Oil on canvas, 28 x 34 in. Private collection. Courtesy of William A. Karges Fine Art

Navajo Riders, after 1929. Oil on canvas, 32 x 40 in. Collection of Charles D. Miller

Burning the Hogan, c. 1930s. Oil on canvas, 28 x 34 in. Courtesy of Arizona West Galleries

Navajo Country, 1942. Oil on canvas, 26 x 35 in. Image courtesy of Bonhams & Butterfield

Untitled [Clouds and Riders], n.d. Oil on canvas, 21½ x 21½ in. Collection of D. L. Stuart Jr.

Two Indians in Southwest Landscape, after 1929. Oil on canvas, 24 x 30 in. Collection of Mr. and Mrs. Thomas B. Stiles II

Blue Canyon, after 1929. Oil on canvas, 34 x 34 in. Private collection

Navajo Stronghold, 1930s. Oil on canvas, 28 x 34 in. Collection of Gilbert and Nancy Waldman

Red Mesa, Monument Valley, Utah, c. 1935. Oil on canvas, 25 x 30 in. Utah Museum of Fine Arts, University of Utah, Salt Lake City, Utah. Purchased with funds from the Phyllis Canon Wattis Endowment for Modern and Contemporary Art, and Diane and Sam Stewart

Monument Valley, 1930s. Oil on canvas, 28 x 34 in. Courtesy of Edenhurst Gallery

Shadowed Butte, n.d. Pencil on paper, 11 x 11 in. Robert Giem Collection

Left: *The Grand Canyon,* n.d. Pencil on paper, 8 x 10½ in. Collection of Mr. and Mrs. Jon R. Stuart

Below: *Stream in the Canyon,* n.d. Pencil on paper, 8 x 10½ in. Collection of Mr. and Mrs. Jon R. Stuart

Canyon de Chelly, n.d. Oil on canvas, 28 x 34 in. Courtesy of the
Springville Museum of Art, Springville, Utah

NOTES

1. "The Editor's Own Page," *Touring Topics* 21 (January 1929): 9.

2. Antony Anderson, "Edgar Payne, Painter and World Traveler," *Laguna Beach South Coast News,* June 21, 1929.

3. Ibid. For a thoughtful discussion of Wendt's mature style and its comparison with Payne's, see William H. Gerdts, "To Light the Landscape," in *California Light, 1900–1930,* ed. Patricia Trenton and William H. Gerdts (Laguna Beach, CA: Laguna Art Museum, 1990), 30.

4. Nancy Dustin Wall Moure, *Dictionary of Art and Artists in Southern California Before 1930,* with introduction by Carl Schaefer Dentzel, Publications in Southern California Art, no. 3 (Glendale, CA: Dustin Publications, 1975).

5. The best sources on Payne and the Southwest are two on which this author has relied heavily: Rena Neumann Coen, *The Paynes, Edgar & Elsie: American Artists* (Minneapolis, MN: Payne Studios, 1988), and A. P. Hays, *Payne's Southwest* (Scottsdale, AZ: Arizona West Galleries, 2000).

6. Elsie Palmer Payne, "Edgar Alwin Payne," unpublished typescript, Edgar and Elsie Palmer Payne Papers, DeRu's Fine Arts, Bellflower, CA. Materials from this source are quoted with the generous permission of Dewitt Clinton McCall III.

7. Newspaper clipping, 1911, Edgar and Elsie Palmer Payne Papers, DeRu's Fine Arts, Bellflower, CA.

8. C. A. Higgins et al., "Titan of Chasms: The Grand Canyon of Arizona," promotional brochure (Chicago: Atchison, Topeka & Santa Fe Railway Company, January 1904).

9. For an account of that trip, see Nina Spalding Stevens, "Pilgrimage to the Artist's Paradise," *Fine Arts Journal* (February 1911): 112.

10. Charles A. Bennett, "Edgar Payne's Beautiful Painting," *Peoria Journal,* May 31, 1914.

11. Ibid.

12. Paul Wakefield, "Texas Boy, Once a 'Sign Dauber,' Becomes a Famous Painter in Oil," *Laguna Beach South Coast News,* March 12, 1916.

13. "I never paint my pictures out of doors," he told a reporter in 1914. "I do them all in the studio. Of course I go out first to gather data on color and composition. I find it easier to humanize a landscape when it is not in front of my eye." "Payne Art Pleasing and Intelligible," *Chicago Daily Tribune,* June 27, 1914.

14. "Art and Artists," Chicago newspaper clipping, Edgar and Elsie Palmer Payne Papers, DeRu's Fine Arts, Bellflower, CA.

15. "Payne Art Pleasing," *Chicago Daily Tribune.* The mayor's brother, Preston, was also an important art collector and purchased two Payne landscapes at the same sale. See Gordon St. Clair, "Edgar Payne's California Paintings," *Inland Stationer,* 1915, 160.

16. A photograph of the visit appears in Rich Morrow, "The Palette & Chisel Academy of Fine Arts," *Cow Bell,* special ed. (2002): 3.

17. Christian Brinton, *Illustrated Catalogue of the Post-Exposition Exhibition in the Department of Fine Arts, Panama-Pacific International Exposition* (San Francisco: San Francisco Art Association, 1915), 109.

18. "Walter Ufer Back from Art Trip," *Chicago Examiner,* November 1915, newspaper clipping in the Palette & Chisel Club scrapbooks, Newberry Library, Chicago.

19. Mary McDonald, interview for KOB Radio, Albuquerque, NM, November 1958, typescript in Ernest Blumenschein Papers, Archives of American Art, Smithsonian Institution, Washington, DC.

20. Walter Ufer, quoted in Paul A. F. Walter, "The Santa Fe–Taos Art Movement," *Art and Archaeology* 4 (December 1916): 330.

21. Ernest Blumenschein, "The Taos Society of Artists," *American Magazine of Art* 11 (September 1917): 451.

22. Richard H. Frost, "The Romantic Inflation of Pueblo Culture," *American West* 17 (January 1980): 5.

23. See Barbara A. Babcock, "First Families: Gender, Reproduction, and the Mythic Southwest," in *The Great Southwest of the Fred Harvey Company and the Santa Fe Railway,* ed. Marta Weigle and Barbara A. Babcock (Phoenix, AZ: Heard Museum, 1996): 209–210.

24. Henry McBride, "War Changes Summer," *New York Sun,* May 17, 1916.

25. *Peoria Journal,* newspaper clipping, March 26, 1916, Edgar and Elsie Palmer Payne Papers, DeRu's Fine Arts, Bellflower, CA.

26. The Edgar and Elsie Palmer Payne Papers contain approximately forty letters and contracts between Payne, Simpson, and others involved in supporting Payne's first summer in Arizona. The following account is taken primarily from those source materials.

27. Roman Hubbell, letter to William H. Simpson, June 25, 1916, Edgar and Elsie Palmer Payne Papers, DeRu's Fine Arts, Bellflower, CA.

28. That the Santa Fe Railway owned just these two Payne paintings in 1917 is confirmed in a letter from F. A. Tipple, general manager, Chicago, to Payne's daughter, Evelyn Hatcher, January 13, 1971, Edgar and Elsie Palmer Payne Papers, DeRu's Fine Arts, Bellflower, CA.

29. Victor Higgins, quoted in J. Kelley, "Real American Art— At Last," *Chicago Sunday Herald*, March 15, 1917.

30. Michael R. Grauer, "Carl Oscar Borg's Niche in American Art," in *Carl Oscar Borg: A Niche in Time; Essays by Katherine Plake Hough, Michael R. Grauer, and Helen Laird* (Palm Springs, CA: Palm Springs Desert Museum, 1990), 28.

31. Willow Roberts Powers, *Navajo Trading: The End of an Era* (Albuquerque: University of New Mexico Press, 2001), 57.

32. *New York Evening World,* September 14, 1917.

33. Coen, *Paynes, Edgar & Elsie,* 64, suggests a trip in 1925, as does Hays, *Payne's Southwest,* 4, but I have been unable to find any evidence of it either in resulting work or in archival references.

34. Mary Marsh, "Art," *Los Angeles Times,* May 29, 1926.

35. "Colorful Vessels . . . and Alpine Crags," newspaper clipping reviewing Payne's 1926 Stendahl Galleries exhibition, Edgar and Elsie Palmer Payne Papers, DeRu's Fine Arts, Bellflower, CA.

36. "Art and Artists," Chicago newspaper clipping, Edgar and Elsie Palmer Payne Papers, DeRu's Fine Arts, Bellflower, CA; Anderson, "Payne, Painter and World Traveler."

37. Eleanor Jewett, "First Shows of the Season Rival the Earlier Offerings in Their Worth and Colorfulness," *Chicago Daily Tribune,* May 25, 1930.

38. Carl Oscar Borg, "The Province of Tusayan," *Touring Topics* 21 (November 1929): 34.

39. Edgar Payne, letter to C. J. Birchfield, May 12, 1934, Edgar and Elsie Palmer Payne Papers, DeRu's Fine Arts, Bellflower, CA.

40. "Payne Canvases Suggest Term, Poems of Color," *Salt Lake Tribune,* July 13, 1930. I am grateful to John Sillito, university archivist and curator of special collections at Weber State University, for providing this reference and other information about Payne's time in Utah.

41. Ibid.

42. *Exhibition of Paintings by Edgar Alwin Payne in the Lounge of [the] Midland Club* (Chicago: Midland Club, May 1931).

43. "News of Arts and Artists," *Chicago Daily Tribune,* May 17, 1931.

44. Hays, *Payne's Southwest,* 7.

45. Edgar A. Payne, *Composition of Outdoor Painting* (Hollywood, CA: Seward, 1941), repr., 7th ed., ed. DeRu's Fine Arts with addenda by Evelyn Payne Hatcher (Bellflower, CA: DeRu's Fine Arts, 2005), 109–110, 117. Page references are to the 2005 edition.

46. Victor Higgins, quoted in Ina Sizer Cassidy, "Art and Artists of New Mexico," *New Mexico Magazine* 10 (December 1932): 22.

47. Payne, *Composition of Outdoor Painting,* 96.

EDGAR PAYNE: PHOTOGRAPHER

Jean Stern

Executive Director
The Irvine Museum

P. 220: *Boats and Rigging, Brittany, France* (detail, p. 226), c. 1928

Above: *Transition from Covered Wagon to Automobile in Navajo Country,* 1920s. Photograph by Edgar Payne. Courtesy of DeRu's Fine Arts

In addition to being an eminent painter, Edgar Payne was a gifted photographer.[1] His daughter and only child, Evelyn Payne Hatcher (1914–2009), confirmed that her father was an avid amateur photographer and that he developed and printed his own photographs.[2] Evelyn remembered watching her father use a detachable bellows in his camera as a surrogate enlarger and print the images in his makeshift darkroom.

Payne took photographs throughout his career. In addition to many personal photographs of his family and their travels, he made images of people and places to use as reference material for his paintings (opposite). Among these are photographs of his family and friends on Santa Cruz Island, one of the dramatic Channel Islands off the coast of Santa Barbara, as well as depictions of the desert Southwest and the Native Americans living there. The vast majority of his extant photographs, however, depict harbor and boat scenes taken in Chioggia, in Italy, and Concarneau, in France. Indeed, of the approximately 200 photographs in the Payne archive, now in the possession of DeRu's Fine Arts in Laguna Beach and Bellflower, California, 183 depict European harbor and boat scenes. His creative mastery of the photographic medium is therefore best seen in this group. Indeed, a good part of the forethought for his book, *Composition of Outdoor Painting* (right), first published in 1941, can be traced directly

to these large-format photographic prints from his European travels. For ease of discussion, these maritime images are hereafter referred to as simply the "boat photographs."

Payne was fascinated by the historic ports of Chioggia and Concarneau. Chioggia is an ancient port located on a small island at the southern entrance to the Venetian Lagoon, off the Adriatic

Edgar Payne's *Composition of Outdoor Painting,* first edition, 1941. Photograph by Jean Stern. Courtesy of Jean Stern

Tuna Yawls, Brittany, France, c. 1928. Photograph by Edgar Payne. Courtesy of DeRu's Fine Arts

coast of Italy. For several centuries, it served as one of Venice's "farm islands" and was the source of much of the food consumed in Venice. Among other commodities, Chioggia furnished large quantities of domestic wine to the island city. At times Payne's Italian boat paintings bear titles such as *Italian Wine Boats* and show the vessels loaded with rows of wine barrels. Payne's other favorite harbor, at Concarneau, is one of the biggest ports in France. Situated on the Brittany coast, it has historically been home to a sizable tuna-fishing fleet (p. 224). In keeping with age-old tradition, the fishermen of Concarneau still use distinctive blue nets to haul in their catch, a color that Payne frequently exploited to bring additional sparkle to his canvases. As Lisa N. Peters also discusses in her essay in this catalogue, Payne spent extended periods at both harbors on a European trip that he took lasting from the summer of 1922 through the summer of 1924.

The majority of the extant boat photographs were probably taken on a shorter European trip lasting from June into September 1928 (pp. 226, 227). In addition to commonality of subject matter, the photographs share other unifying factors. All were printed on similarly textured lightweight photographic paper measuring 14 by 11 inches, perhaps an indication that they were printed at the same time. Moreover, of the 183 images that exist in the Payne archive, 46 of them were backed with torn-out pages from issues of the *Saturday Evening Post*. Most of the pages were from issues dated 1928, a few were dated 1927, and even fewer backings were dated 1929.

The dating on the torn-out magazine pages is significant in that it is much closer in time to the Paynes' 1928 trip. Their first trip to Europe, starting in 1922, took them to France and Italy. Over the two years of their visit, they traveled to Paris; the French Alps; Menton, France; Rome; Venice and Chioggia; Interlaken, Switzerland; and finally Brittany and London before returning to the United States. By contrast, the second trip, in 1928, lasted only three months and was for the expressed purpose of gathering material for future boat paintings. After arriving in France, the Paynes headed for Chioggia. They ended their trip in Brittany, where the Paynes were joined by their friend and fellow Laguna Beach artist George Brandriff.

While the Paynes had ample time to produce large numbers of plein-air sketches on their twenty-six-month trip in 1922, they had fewer opportunities to do so on the short 1928 trip. Instead, Payne relied on his camera to record the scenes that he would later paint. It is unknown exactly what type of camera and photographic equipment Payne took to Europe. There were no cameras extant in the estates of Edgar and Elsie Payne, and Evelyn could not recall what type of camera her father used, though she did remember that it had folding bellows and could be converted to function as an enlarger. Kodak had pioneered the manufacture of simple, easy-to-use handheld cameras as early as 1900, the year the Brownie line was introduced. By the mid-1920s, amateur photography had been generally available to the public for more than two decades, although the quality of cameras and film was still rather basic. The concept of using a handheld camera presupposed that the resulting image would be small, grainy, and very likely blurred because of the slow speed of film and shutter. Yet the high quality and composition of the boat photographs preclude the notion that Payne could have used an

Boats and Rigging, Brittany, France, c. 1928. Photograph by Edgar Payne. Courtesy of DeRu's Fine Arts

Going to the Boats, Brittany, France, c. 1928. Photograph by Edgar Payne. Courtesy of DeRu's Fine Arts

ordinary portable camera of the day; he would have needed an advanced camera and a tripod to steady his shots and eliminate blurring. Very few of the photographs show any blurring and the focus is sharp and steady, even though the photographs were enlarged to at least four times the size of the negatives. The excellent quality of the boat pictures testifies to a much more advanced system of photography.

By the mid-1920s, Kodak was manufacturing a number of popular cameras suited to the amateur photographer. Some of these cameras were elementary and simple, while others had options for the advanced amateur. One of the more versatile Kodak cameras available throughout this period was the model 3A series, produced from 1916 to 1934 (below left). A large and popular line of cameras, the

3A used Kodak's size 122 film, sold either in rolls or in preloaded sheets. The negative measured 3¼ by 5½ inches and was called the "postcard" size. Kodak 122 film was the largest format made for amateur use.

For the truly advanced amateur, the 3A could be fitted with an optional combination back (below right). This back was available at extra cost and featured a ground-glass panel. The standard back was easily removed from the camera and replaced with the combination back. While the 3A would utilize roll film when used with the standard back, the combination back required the use of size 122 sheet film, which was sold in bulk or preloaded, two sheets at a time, in lightproof film holders.

With the combination back, the operator could look through the ground glass and see directly

Above left: Advertisement for Kodak model 3A Autographic camera. Courtesy of Jean Stern

Above right: Kodak model 3A camera with combination back. Courtesy of Jean Stern

through the lens opening, an expedience that allowed for exact composition and much greater accuracy in focusing the camera. To take a picture, the operator would need to mount the camera on a sturdy tripod or other support and, while looking through the ground-glass back, compose the shot and focus the image. A piece of dark fabric draped over the operator and the back of the camera would make viewing the image easier. Next, the operator would affix a pre-loaded film holder onto two brackets located against the ground-glass back, pull out the lightproof panel on the side of the film holder facing the ground glass, click the shutter, replace the lightproof panel, and remove the film holder from the combination back. To limit the chance that the camera would shake when the operator manually released the shutter, the Kodak 3A came equipped with a rubber squeeze-bulb shutter release. The entire process would be repeated to take a picture with the second sheet of film housed in the other side of the film holder. Although there is no way to confirm that Payne used a Kodak model 3A, it seems doubtful that he could have produced his high-quality photographs without this camera or one very much like it.

That Payne used photographs to compose his paintings cannot be denied. However, it is important to understand that he used his photographs as trial pieces for compositional purposes and not for the enlargement of an image to be transferred to a canvas prior to painting. If Payne had indeed enlarged his photos for transferring onto a blank canvas, the photographs would most likely have had a superimposed grid of pencil lines, similar to graph paper. None of the 183 photographs bears grid lines. Moreover, his canvases would have included grids for transferring the

images. In a series of photographs of Payne at work in his Paris studio taken in 1924, he is shown painting a 62 by 62 inch view of Mont Blanc (see p. 144) with a small plein-air sketch of Mont Blanc affixed to the upper left edge of his canvas. Clearly, Payne is using a small plein-air sketch to guide himself in the large studio work, but neither the sketch nor the canvas shows any grid pattern. Payne employed his photographs in a similar manner.

In addition to their use in future paintings, the collection of boat photographs served as concrete demonstrations of Payne's ideas about composition—ideas that would later be published in his book, *Composition of Outdoor Painting*. Through photography, Payne was able to encapsulate his approaches to composition and to deliberate differing procedures easier and faster than with actual paintings. A natural extension of his musings on composition, the boat photographs unmistakably show many of Payne's basic compositional forms and structures, such as the pyramid, diagonal, cross, radiating line, silhouette, and steelyard. The photographs therefore offer both a direct testimony to Payne's mastery of the medium and a glimpse into his creative process.

NOTES

1. In September 2010, I examined a collection of nearly two hundred various photographs taken by Edgar Payne, now in the possession of Dewitt Clinton McCall III of DeRu's Fine Arts in Laguna Beach and Bellflower, California. As the longtime representative of the estates of Edgar A. Payne and his wife, Elsie Palmer Payne, McCall obtained the photographs from the Paynes' daughter, Evelyn Payne Hatcher.

2. This information was related by Evelyn Payne Hatcher to Dewitt McCall.

CHRONOLOGY

1883 March 1: Edgar Alwin Payne is born near Cassville, Barry County, Missouri; he is the second child and first son of John Hill Payne and Nancy Ellen Reed Payne, who will ultimately have six sons and two daughters

1884 September 9: Elsie Palmer is born in San Antonio, Texas

1894 Payne family moves to Prairie Grove, Arkansas, where Edgar's mother has inherited property

Edgar Payne makes his first attempts at painting

1900 Summer: Payne family moves to Lovelady, Texas

Payne begins painting signs

1902 Paints scenery in the town hall in Lovelady and at the high school in Conroe, Texas

1902–1903 Leaves home and travels, supporting himself with painting jobs (fences, barns, signs, etc.)

1903 Travels with a theatrical troupe, paints and rigs scenery, works as a handyman, and occasionally performs

1905–1906 Moves to Houston and sets up housekeeping with his sisters, Fleda and Nora

Paints signs and houses, hangs wallpaper, and works at a scene-painting shop

1906 Sets up a scene-painting shop—Payne-Morris Studios—in Dallas

1907 April 1: Enrolls in a portrait-painting class at the Art Institute of Chicago; drops out after two weeks

Receives critiques from Chicago artists Ralph Clarkson and Charles Francis Browne

1908 Payne's parents separate

1909 Payne makes his first trip to California and visits Laguna Beach

Meets Elsie Palmer in San Francisco

Exhibits a watercolor in the Chicago Palette & Chisel Club's *Exhibition of Illustrating and Advertising Art*

May–June: Exhibits *Landscape* (watercolor) at the Art Institute of Chicago's *Twenty-First Annual Exhibition of Water-Colors, Pastels and Miniatures by American Artists* (address listed: 22 Studio Building, Chicago)

1910 January: Exhibits *A Sunny Hillside* at the Art Institute of Chicago's *Fourteenth Annual Exhibition of Works by Chicago Artists* (address listed: 26 East Van Buren Street, Chicago)

April: United States Census lists Payne's residence as 3 East Ontario Street, dwelling 23, Chicago; artist C. Bertram Hartman (1882–1960) and lodger C. Wilbraut are also listed at this address

May: Exhibits *The Sierra del Burro Mountains, Mexico* (watercolor) at the Art Institute of Chicago's *Twenty Second Annual Exhibition of Water-Colors, Pastels and Miniatures by American Artists* (address listed: 25 Tree Studio Building, Chicago)

May–June: Holds an exhibition at the Palette & Chisel Club, Chicago

1911 January: Exhibits *November Woods* and *The Golden Autumn* at the Art Institute of Chicago's *Fifteenth Annual Exhibition of Works by Chicago Artists* (address listed: 25 Tree Studio Building, Chicago)

Spends four months scene painting in the Edwin Flagg Studio, Los Angeles

Summer: Visits Santa Catalina Island, Laguna Canyon, and Laguna Beach; paints his first marines of the Laguna Beach coast, including *Laguna Beach Coast, Low Tide,* and *The Little Cove*

Goes on sketching excursions with Hanson Puthuff and Norman St. Clair

Returns to Chicago

Wins a prize for a California landscape at the Palette & Chisel Club, Chicago

1911–1912 Elsie Palmer is in Chicago, working for Clague Advertising

Payne makes hand-carved picture frames at The Studio Frame Shop, Chicago, with partners Louis Grosse and O. Irwin Myers

Pursues mural painting and decorative work through the Payne-Kratzner Studios

1912 February: Exhibits *The Patriarch of the Canyon, Shadows in the Canyon, The Bay of Avalon,* and *The Day of the Aviation* at the Art Institute of Chicago's *Sixteenth Annual Exhibition of Works by Chicago Artists* (address listed: 20 Tree Studio Building, Chicago)

Opposite: *Sunflowers,* n.d. Oil on canvas, 22 x 18 in. J. Dutra Collection

March: Holds an exhibition of Southern California paintings at the Palette & Chisel Club, Chicago

Paints murals for theaters and courthouses in the Midwest

November 9: Marries Elsie Palmer in Chicago

November–December: Exhibits *The Hills of El Toro* at the Art Institute of Chicago's *Twenty-Fifth Annual Exhibition of American Sculpture and Oil Paintings* (address listed: Tree Studio Building, Chicago)

1913 Becomes a member of the Paris-based Union internationale des beaux-arts et des lettres

January 14: Painting of Laguna Canyon, *Western Hills,* wins $100 prize at the Tingel-Tangel of the Palette & Chisel Club, Chicago

January–February: Exhibits *A Western Valley* at the Art Institute of Chicago's *Seventeenth Annual Exhibition of Works by Artists of Chicago and Vicinity* (address listed: 4 East Ohio Street, Chicago)

March: Holds an exhibition of sixty-five small California landscapes at the Palette & Chisel Club, Chicago

March–April: Exhibits *An Idyll* (watercolor) and a decorative panel (watercolor) at the Art Institute of Chicago's *Twenty-Fifth Annual Exhibition of Water Colors, Pastels and Miniatures by American Artists* (address listed: 4 East Ohio Street, Chicago)

Summer: Makes a sketching trip to California and paints in Marin County

November–December: Exhibits *Hills Eternal: Mt. Lowe* at the Art Institute of Chicago's *Twenty-Sixth Annual Exhibition of American Paintings and Sculpture* (address listed: Tree Studio Building, Chicago)

Receives a commission from the Mitchell and Holbeck Company of Chicago to create a mural for the Hendricks County Courthouse, Danville, Indiana

1914 January 12: Daughter, Evelyn, is born in Chicago

February: Exhibits *Sausalito Hills, The Hills of Marin, Hillside Shadows,* and a decorative watercolor panel at the Art Institute of Chicago's *Eighteenth Annual Exhibition of Works by Artists of Chicago and Vicinity* (address listed: 4 East Ohio Street, Chicago)

Contributes to an exhibition of Chicago artists held by the Peoria Society of Allied Arts, a chapter of the American Federation of Arts; the society purchases *The Hills of Marin* and hangs it in the Peoria Public Library

Completes murals for the Hendricks County Courthouse, Danville, Indiana, and the Clay County Courthouse, Brazil, Indiana

Completes murals for the American Theater, Chicago; the project includes a sixty-foot allegorical mural, *Progress,* over the proscenium arch

May–June: Exhibits *Spring* (watercolor) and a decorative panel (watercolor) at the Art Institute of Chicago's *Twenty-Sixth Annual Exhibition of Water Colors, Pastels and Miniatures by American Artists* (address listed: 4 East Ohio Street, Chicago)

June–July: Shows eighty landscapes in a joint exhibition with sculptor Nancy Cox-McCormack at the Palette & Chisel Club, Chicago; Chicago's mayor, Carter H. Harrison Jr., purchases two small landscapes

Summer: Makes a sketching trip to California

Summer–fall: Paints murals for the Queen Theater, Houston; stays with sister

November–December: Exhibits *Hills Aglow* and *Sespe Canyon* at the Art Institute of Chicago's *Twenty-Seventh Annual Exhibition of American Oil Paintings and Sculpture* (address listed: 4 East Ohio Street, Chicago)

1915 March: Holds an exhibition at the Palette & Chisel Club, Chicago

March: Exhibits *Peaceful Valley* and *A Verdugo Morning* at the Art Institute of Chicago's *Nineteenth Annual Exhibition of Works by Artists of Chicago and Vicinity* (address listed: 4 East Ohio Street, Chicago)

May–June: Exhibits a decorative watercolor panel at the Art Institute of Chicago's *Twenty-Seventh Annual Exhibition of Water Colors, Pastels and Miniatures by American Artists* (address listed: 4 East Ohio Street, Chicago)

Summer: Travels to San Francisco to visit Elsie's family and see the Panama-Pacific International

Exposition; exhibits *Infinitude* in the fine arts section of the exposition and *Dewy Eve* in the Illinois State Building

Summer: Travels to Santa Barbara to sketch and paint; visits the Channel Islands

Holds an exhibition with O. Irwin Myers at the Kalos studio, City Hall Plaza, Santa Barbara

1915–1916 November–January: Exhibits *The Coast at Valdez* and *La Cumbre Slopes* at the Art Institute of Chicago's *Twenty-Eighth Annual Exhibition of American Oil Paintings and Sculpture* (address listed: 4 East Ohio Street, Chicago)

1916 January: Participates in the *Thumb Box Exhibition* at the Palette & Chisel Club, Chicago

February–March: Exhibits *The Rendezvous, The Santa Ynez,* and *Vista at Montrose* at the Art Institute of Chicago's *Twentieth Annual Exhibition of Works by Artists of Chicago and Vicinity* (address listed: 4 East Ohio Street, Chicago)

Joins The Trailers, a club of painters who have joined together to visit the wonders of the West and hold a show upon their return; he is elected first vice president of the organization but does not make the trip

March: Exhibits *The Rendezvous* at the Palette & Chisel Club, Chicago

March: With Walter Ufer and Carl Krafft, organizes a Palette & Chisel Club exhibition that travels to Peoria, Illinois; St. Louis, Missouri; and Lexington, Kentucky

Spring: Exhibits *California Hills* and *Western Foothills* at the National Academy of Design, New York (address listed: 4 East Ohio Street, Chicago)

April: Holds an exhibition at the Palette & Chisel Club, Chicago, with painter E. Martin Hennings and sculptor Maximilian Hoffman

April–May: Exhibits *The Island Coast, Monteceito Way, Hills of Rincon,* and *Vista, Santa Barbara* at the Art Institute of Chicago's *Twenty-First Annual Exhibition of the Palette & Chisel Club*

May: Holds an exhibition of California landscapes and coastal scenes at the Moulton and Ricketts Art Galleries, Chicago

May–June: Exhibits *Fantasy* (watercolor) at the Art Institute of Chicago's *Twenty-Eighth Annual*

Exhibition of Water Colors, Pastels and Miniatures by American Artists (no address listed)

Summer: Visits New Mexico, Arizona, and other places in the Southwest; transportation is provided by the Atchison, Topeka & Santa Fe Railway Company (Santa Fe Railway)

June 25: Arrives in Gallup, New Mexico

Late June: Visits Canyon de Chelly

July–October 15: Lives on and near Navajo and Hopi reservations

October 15: Arrives at El Tovar

Fall: Returns to Chicago

Winter: Exhibits *Coward's Cove* at the National Academy of Design, New York (address listed: 4 East Ohio Street, Chicago)

November–December: Exhibits *Mountain Mist* and *Sea Foam* at the Art Institute of Chicago's *Twenty-Ninth Annual Exhibition of American Oil Paintings and Sculpture* (address listed: 4 East Ohio Street, Chicago)

Paints *The Restless Sea*

1917 February–March: Exhibits *Sea and Rocks, No. II* ($200), *Navajo Country* ($300), *A Navajo Pastoral* ($500), *A Valley Vista* ($250), *The Coast at Laguna* ($500), and *The Restless Sea* ($500) at the Art Institute of Chicago's *Twenty-First Annual Exhibition of Works by Artists of Chicago and Vicinity* (address listed: 4 East Ohio Street, Chicago); *The Restless Sea* is purchased for the John Herron Art Institute of Indianapolis

March: Santa Fe Railway acquires *Sunset, Canyon de Chelly* and *Navajo Country*

Spring: Payne exhibits *Seafoam* at the National Academy of Design, New York (address listed: 4 East Ohio Street, Chicago)

May–June: Exhibits *Seascape* (watercolor, $100) and *Decorative Panel, No. 5* (watercolor, $75) at the Art Institute of Chicago's *Twenty-Ninth Annual Exhibition of Water Colors, Pastels and Miniatures by American Artists* (address listed: 4 East Ohio Street, Chicago)

Holds an exhibition of thirty-five paintings at Diamond Disc shop, Peoria, Illinois; delivers a series of gallery talks in conjunction with the exhibition

July: Accepts a mural commission from Holslag & Company of Chicago for the Congress Hotel, Michigan Avenue, Chicago

Summer: Moves to Glendale, California, to work on Congress Hotel murals; rents a piano factory in Tropico (now Glendale)

Hires friends Peter Nielsen, Jack Wilkinson Smith, Fred Grayson Sayre, and, later, Conrad Buff to help paint murals

October: Exhibits *Pasadena Mountains* at the Los Angeles Museum of History, Science, and Art's *Eighth Annual Exhibition of the California Art Club*

November: Completes murals, moves to Laguna Beach, and rents a home

1917 or 1918   Makes his first Sierra Nevada trip

1918   Purchases and then extensively remodels a studio-home on Glenneyre Street, Laguna Beach

Becomes a guiding figure in the establishment of the Laguna Beach Art Association and gallery

Exhibits *Arch Beach Coast* and *Restless Waters* at the California Liberty Fair, Los Angeles; wins honorable mention

April: Exhibits *High Tide* and *Rock Bound* at the Los Angeles Museum of History, Science, and Art's *Spring Exhibition of the California Art Club*

July 27: Old town hall in Laguna Beach opens as an art gallery

August: Payne's father dies

August 15: Organizational meeting of the Laguna Beach Art Association is held at Payne's Laguna Beach home; Payne is elected first president, Anna Hills first vice president

September: Wins a gold medal at the California State Fair art exhibition, Sacramento

September 7: Registers for the draft, Orange County, California

September–October: Exhibits *Rocks and Sea* and *Heavy Sea* at the Los Angeles Museum of History, Science, and Art's *Ninth Annual Exhibition of the California Art Club*

November–December: Exhibits *Rising Tide* at the Art Institute of Chicago's *Thirty-First Annual Exhibition of American Oil Paintings and Sculpture* (address listed: 4 East Ohio Street, Chicago)

1919   February–March: Exhibits *Angry Sea* at the Art Institute of Chicago's *Twenty-Third Annual Exhibition of Works by Artists of Chicago and Vicinity* (address listed: 4 East Ohio Street, Chicago)

March: Holds an exhibition of coastal scenes and marines at Exposition Park, Los Angeles

April: Exhibits *California Vista* at the Los Angeles Museum of History, Science, and Art's *Spring Exhibition of the California Art Club*

Summer: Sketches in the Sierra; paints *Rugged Slopes and Tamarack*

Fall: Returns to Laguna Beach

September: Wins a silver medal at the California State Fair art exhibition, Sacramento

October: Exhibits *Sierra Slopes* and *Sierra Pines* at the Los Angeles Museum of History, Science, and Art's *Tenth Annual Exhibition of the California Art Club*

November–December: Exhibits *The High Sierras* and *Timber Line* at the Art Institute of Chicago's *Thirty-Second Annual Exhibition of American Oil Paintings and Sculpture* (address listed: 4 East Ohio Street, Chicago)

1920   February: Holds an exhibition of eighteen landscapes and coastal scenes at Cannell and Chaffin, Los Angeles

February–March: Exhibits *The Topmost Peak, Wooded Slopes,* and *Rocky Shore* at the Art Institute of Chicago's *Twenty-Fourth Annual Exhibition of Works by Artists of Chicago and Vicinity* (address listed: 867 North Dearborn Street, Chicago)

October–November: Exhibits *Upper Lake* and *Eternal Surge* at the Los Angeles Museum of History, Science, and Art's *Eleventh Annual Exhibition of the California Art Club*

November: Awarded the Martin B. Cahn Prize ($100) for *Rugged Slopes and Tamarack* at the Art Institute of Chicago's *Thirty-Third Annual Exhibition of American Oil Paintings and Sculpture* (address listed: 867 North Dearborn Street, Chicago)

Completes his term as president of the Laguna Beach Art Association

Moves from Laguna Beach to Los Angeles

1921 January–February: Exhibits *Laguna Waters* ($500), *Eternal Surge* ($800), and *The Topmost Sierras* ($1,000) at the Art Institute of Chicago's *Twenty-Fifth Annual Exhibition of Works by Artists of Chicago and Vicinity* (address listed: 867 North Dearborn Street, Chicago)

January–February: Holds an exhibition at the gallery of O'Hara and Livermore, Pasadena

February: Exhibits *Rugged Slopes and Tamarack* at the Pennsylvania Academy of the Fine Arts, Philadelphia (address listed: 867 North Dearborn Street, Chicago)

February–March: Holds an exhibition at the Stendahl Galleries, Ambassador Hotel, Los Angeles

April: Holds an exhibition at Orr's Art Gallery, San Diego

Receives first prize for *Topmost Crags* from the Southwest Museum in Huntington Park, California

Summer: Sketches in the Sierra

October–November: Exhibits *Rugged Slopes and Tamarack* at the Los Angeles Museum of History, Science, and Art's *Twelfth Annual Exhibition of the California Art Club*

November–December: Exhibits *Slopes of Leevining [Lee Vining]* (price handwritten in catalogue: $2,000) at the Art Institute of Chicago's *Thirty-Fourth Annual Exhibition of American Paintings and Sculpture* (address listed: 867 North Dearborn Street, Chicago)

1922 February: Exhibits *Solitude's Enchantment* at the Pennsylvania Academy of the Fine Arts, Philadelphia (address listed: 867 North Dearborn Street, Chicago)

February: Holds an exhibition at the Stendahl Galleries, Ambassador Hotel, Los Angeles

February–March: Exhibits *Rugged Slopes and Tamarack* in the *Selected Work by Western Painters Annual Traveling Exhibition,* organized by the Kansas City Art Institute and the Western Association of Art Museum Directors

May: Painting *Sierra Ruggedness* is gifted to the Southwest Museum, Huntington Park, California, by James Slauson of Santa Monica

May 22: Honored at a banquet held at the Stendahl Galleries just before his departure for Europe

June: Stops in Chicago en route to New York

July: Exhibits at Grace Hickox's studio, Fine Arts Building, Chicago

July: Sails from New York to Paris; reaches Paris in late July

August 22: Receives automobile license; address is listed as 21, rue d'Athènes, Paris (address of Hôtel d'Athènes)

August: Visits battlefields of World War I; drives down the Chamonix Valley, visiting Saint-Gervais-les-Bains, Les Contamines, and Argentière; visits Switzerland

September: Wins first prize for *Silvery Light, Laguna* at the California State Fair art exhibition, Sacramento

September: Leaves Paris for the French Alps; probably stays in the town of Chamonix and travels through the Haute-Savoie

October: Leaves the French Alps, heading toward Marseilles and visiting Monaco, Nice, Cannes, Antibes, Juan-les-Pins, and Menton, on the Italian border, and then crosses into Italy and spends time on the Ligurian coast, visiting Rapallo and Santa Margherita

1922–1923 November–March: Winters in Rome in an apartment and studio on the Piazza Dante

Finishes his first painting of Mont Blanc, *Le Grand Pic Blanc*

1923 March: Leaves Rome for Switzerland; visits Tivoli, Perugia, Florence, Genoa, and other towns and then travels past Lake Maggiore and on to Domodossola; in Florence, visits the Uffizi Gallery and the Palazzo Pitti

April: In Brig, Switzerland, and then visits Lake Geneva, where it is too cold for sketching; travels by train to Venice, Italy

April–May: Holds an exhibition of twenty-six paintings of the Swiss Alps, the French Alps, the French Riviera, and the Italian Riviera at the Stendahl Galleries, Ambassador Hotel, Los Angeles

May: Exhibits two paintings at the Paris Salon, *Les Hauts [sic] Sierra (California)* and *Le Grand Pic Blanc (The Great White Peak);* receives honorable mention for *Le Grand Pic Blanc*

Summer: Travels to Chioggia, Italy

Returns to Switzerland

Sketches at Lake Lucerne and in the Engelberg Valley; stays at the Hotel Krebs Interlaken, a base for painting Spiez Castle on the south shore of the Thunersee, the Wellhorn, Grindelwald, the Wetterhorn, the Eiger, Mürren, and the Jungfrau (all in the Bernese Alps); paints the Matterhorn in Zermatt (in the Pennine Alps)

July 1: Travels to Paris to receive honorable mention from the Paris Salon for *Le Grand Pic Blanc*

July–August: Holds an exhibition at the Maryland Galleries, Pasadena

July–August: Holds an exhibition at the Stendahl Galleries, Ambassador Hotel, Los Angeles

Late September: Returns to Paris and resides at 48, rue Vavin, with a studio located at 51, boulevard Saint-Jacques, both on the Left Bank

Visits Salon d'Automne, Paris

Joins American Art Association of Paris

November–December: Exhibits *California Sierras* (price handwritten in catalogue: $2,000) at the Art Institute of Chicago's *Thirty-Sixth Annual Exhibition of American Paintings and Sculpture* (address listed: 867 North Dearborn Street, Chicago)

December: Holds an exhibition of landscapes of California and Europe at the Ebell Club, Los Angeles

1923–1924 Winters in Paris at 48, rue Vavin

November–May: Exhibits *Sunlit Peaks, The High Alps, The Ligurian Coast, Adriatic Boats,* and *Boats of Chioggia* in the *Second Biennial Roman International Exposition,* held at the Palazzo di Belle Arti on the via Nazionale, Rome

1924 January–February: Exhibits with the American Art Association of Paris; works include *Boats, Chioggia* and *Glacier*

Exhibits in the Venice International Exhibition

February–March: Exhibits *Les Haut Sierra* (price

handwritten in catalogue: $2,000) and *Le Grand Pic Blanc* (handwritten in catalogue: $2,000) at the Art Institute of Chicago's *Twenty-Eighth Annual Exhibition by Artists of Chicago and Vicinity* (no address listed)

February–March: Visits the *Second Biennial Roman International Exposition*

Paints *The Great White Peak* (a larger version of *Le Grand Pic Blanc*) in his Paris studio

March–April: Shows sixteen works in a joint exhibition with sculptor Nancy Cox-McCormack at the Galeries Jacques Seligmann et fils, former château de Sagan, 57, rue Saint-Dominique, Paris

April: Travels to Venice in the company of Cornelius Botke and George Evans

April: Exhibits *Alpine Vista* at the Los Angeles Museum of History, Science, and Art's *Painters and Sculptors, Fifth Annual Exhibition*

May 1: Exhibits *Le Monarque des Oberland (La Jungfrau),* no. 1509, and *Les Hauteurs* (also known as *Snow Clad Heights,* a view of the Wellhorn), no. 1510, at the Paris Salon, organized by the Société des artistes français (address listed: 48, rue Vavin, Paris)

Summer: Sketches in the Loire Valley (châteaux de Montrésor and Loches), in Brittany (châteaux de Josselin and Combourg, near Saint-Malo), and on the Brittany coast; spends extended time in Concarneau and Douarnenez, visits Camaret, and travels to Mont Saint-Michel in Normandy

Late summer: Spends two weeks in London; visits museums

September 16: Leaves for New York on the SS *Leviathan*

September 22: Arrives at the Port of New York

December: Exhibits at Cannell and Chaffin, Los Angeles

1924–1925 Fall–winter: In Chicago

1925 February: Exhibits *Sails of Cameret [sic]* and *The White Dome* at the Pennsylvania Academy of the Fine Arts, Philadelphia (address listed: 867 North Dearborn Street, Chicago)

February–March: Exhibits *Bernese Peaks* and *Tuna Fishermen* at the Art Institute of Chicago's *Twenty-*

Ninth Annual Exhibition by Artists of Chicago and Vicinity (no address listed)

March–April: Holds an exhibition at the Newcomb Macklin & Co. galleries, Chicago

May: Drives to California accompanied by George Hurrell; in an automobile accident near Denver, Colorado

June: Visits Laguna Beach; holds an exhibition in Buck Weaver's studio

July: Visits San Francisco

July–August: Sketches in the Sierra

August–September: Wins a prize for *Tuna Fisherman, Concarneau* in an exhibition of the Laguna Beach Art Association

September: Wins second prize for *The Harbor* at the California State Fair art exhibition, Sacramento

October: Wins a gold medal for best landscape for *Peaks and Shadows* at the Los Angeles Museum of History, Science, and Art's *Sixteenth Annual Exhibition of the California Art Club*

Late fall: Establishes a residence at 134 South Reno Street, Los Angeles, and a studio at 550 South New Hampshire Avenue

November: Holds an exhibition at the Thomas Whipple Dunbar Galleries, Chicago

November–December: Exhibits *Border Peaks* (price handwritten in catalogue: $2,000) at the Art Institute of Chicago's *Thirty-Eighth Annual Exhibition of American Paintings and Sculpture* (no address listed)

1926 April: Wins the Tingley Memorial bronze medal from the Painters and Sculptors Club of Los Angeles, of which he is a member

May: Exhibits *The Return* at Cannell and Chaffin, Los Angeles

May–June: Holds a retrospective exhibition of sixty canvases and two model boats at the Stendahl Galleries, Ambassador Hotel, Los Angeles; exhibition includes an illustrated hardbound catalogue with a biography and appreciation by Antony Anderson and an essay by Fred S. Hogue

Becomes president of the California Art Club

Summer: Sketches and paints in the Sierra

September: Exhibits at the California State Fair, Sacramento

October: Moves to Westport, Connecticut; rents the Bean Studio on Kings Highway

1927 April: Organizes an exhibition for the Women's Town Improvement Association in the YMCA of Westport, Connecticut

April: Leaves Westport for Chicago and then California; Elsie and Evelyn remain behind

April–May: Exhibits *The Home Port* at the Los Angeles Museum of History, Science, and Art's *Painters and Sculptors, Eighth Annual Exhibition*

May–June: Holds an exhibition at the Stendahl Galleries, Ambassador Hotel, Los Angeles

June–July: Holds an exhibition at the Chicago Galleries Association, Chicago

July: Holds an exhibition at the Ebell Club, Los Angeles

July: Contributes to the Laguna Beach Art Association's *Building Fund Exhibition,* held at Saint Ann's Inn, Santa Ana, California

Summer: Sketches in the Sierra

August 7: Receives a commission for eight large murals for the Hotel St. Paul, Los Angeles

Fall: Moves to Spuyten Duyvil, in the Riverdale section of the Bronx, New York (address listed in 1930 census: 3129 Netherland Avenue, Bronx); has a studio on Broadway

October–November: Contracts pneumonia and is confined to his apartment; paints gouaches at home

1928 Becomes a member of the Salmagundi Club and The American Artists Professional League

January: Holds an exhibition with Dedrick Stuber at Wilshire Galleries, Los Angeles

Visits Ogden, Utah, in preparation for an exhibition the following July; holds an exhibition at the Hotel Utah, Salt Lake City

Spring: Exhibits *Chioggia Boats* and *The Inyo Sierra* at the National Academy of Design, New York (address listed: 1931 Broadway, New York)

June 9: Leaves for Europe from New York on the SS *Minnekahda,* arrives in Paris, and travels to Chioggia, Brittany, and the Riviera

Summer: Construction begins on the new art gallery of the Laguna Beach Art Association

July 24: Registers a Model T Ford with the Préfet du département d'Alpes Maritimes in Nice, France; address is listed as 8, boulevard Caracael, Nice

July–August: Exhibits at the Hotel Bigelow, Ogden, Utah

July–August: Exhibits in the Pacific Southwest Exposition, Long Beach, California

July–August: Holds an exhibition with Maurice Braun at the Bartlett Galleries, Los Angeles

August: Wins second prize for *Granite Slopes* in an exhibition of the Laguna Beach Art Association

August–September: Exhibits *Sunlight Cliffs near Bridgeport* at the Pasadena Public Library

September 15: Leaves for New York from Boulogne-sur-Mer aboard the SS *Minnekahda*

September 24: Arrives at the Port of New York

November 23–December 14: Exhibits *Fishing Boats* in the *Annual Exhibition of Water Colors, Pastels and Wax Color Crayons* at the Salmagundi Club, New York

December: Exhibits at the Roosevelt Hotel, Hollywood, California

December: *Fifth Lake* is acquired by the National Academy of Design through the Henry Ward Ranger Purchase Fund

Winter: Exhibits *Tuna Boats* and *Fifth Lake* at the National Academy of Design, New York (address listed: 1931 Broadway, New York)

1929 January: Exhibits at the Woman's Club of Hollywood

January 18–31: Exhibits *Sierra Lake* in the *Annual Auction Sale* at the Salmagundi Club, New York

February 15: Contributes to the opening exhibition in the new gallery of the Laguna Beach Art Association

March 8–22: Exhibits *Boats of Sottomarina* in the *Annual Exhibition of Oil Paintings* at the Salmagundi Club, New York

Spring: Travels to Los Angeles via Chicago and Ogden, Utah

Spring: Exhibits *The Alps at Kandersteg* and *Anchorage* at the National Academy of Design, New York (address listed: 1931 Broadway, New York)

April: Exhibits at the Laguna Beach Art Association

May: Holds an exhibition at the Allerton Galleries, Chicago

May–June: Holds an exhibition at the Bartlett Galleries, Los Angeles

June: Holds an exhibition at the Hotel Bigelow, Ogden, Utah

June: Holds an exhibition of twenty-six paintings at the Biltmore Salon, Biltmore Hotel, Los Angeles

July: Departs from Laguna Beach for a sketching trip in the Canadian Rockies

July: Holds an exhibition of watercolors at the Bartlett Galleries, Los Angeles

September: Exhibits at the Biltmore Salon, Biltmore Hotel, Los Angeles

Fall: Returns to New York

October: Exhibits *The Wetterhorn* (in the collection of Harry C. Bentley), with other paintings by Southern California artists, at the Copley Gallery, Boston

October: Exhibits *Fifth Lake* in the *Ranger Exhibition* at the National Gallery of Art, Washington, DC

November 22–December 13: Exhibits *Boats from Camaret* in the *Annual Exhibition of Water Colors, Pastels and Wax Color Crayons* at the Salmagundi Club, New York

December: Included in the group exhibition *Masters of the West* at the Stendahl Galleries, Ambassador Hotel, Los Angeles

Winter: Exhibits *Chioggia Sails* and *Peaks: Moraine Lake* at the National Academy of Design, New York (address listed: 1931 Broadway, New York)

1930 Serves on the Art Committee of the Salmagundi Club, New York

March: Exhibits *Cargo Boats (Chioggia, Italy)* at the Ebell Club, Los Angeles

March 7–28: Exhibits *Shadowed Peaks* in the *Annual Exhibition of Oil Paintings* at the Salmagundi Club, New York

Spring: Exhibits *Breton Sails* and *Mount Burgess* at the National Academy of Design, New York (address listed: 1931 Broadway, New York)

Spring: Travels from New York to Chicago

May: Holds an exhibition at the Illinois Women's Athletic Club, Chicago

Summer: Holds an exhibition in the gallery of the new Architecture Building at the University of Illinois

July: Travels to Ogden, Utah

July: Holds an exhibition at the Hotel Utah, Salt Lake City

July: Travels to Zion and Bryce Canyons with Buck Weaver

July–August: Travels to Thoreau, New Mexico, and then Gallup, New Mexico; returns to Thoreau

August: Holds an exhibition at the Ainslie Gallery, Los Angeles

1930–1931 Late fall–winter: Lives in New York

1931 Serves on the Art Committee of the Salmagundi Club, New York

February 13–27: Exhibits *Evening, Arizona* in the *Annual Exhibition of Water Colors, Pastels and Wax Color Crayons* at the Salmagundi Club, New York

March 6–22: Exhibits *Desert Trail* in the *Annual Exhibition of Oil Paintings* at the Salmagundi Club, New York

Spring: Exhibits *Palisade Glacier* and *Desert Nomads* at the National Academy of Design, New York (address listed: 1931 Broadway, New York)

May–June: Holds an exhibition of thirty-four paintings in the lounge of the Midland Club, Chicago

May 15–October 10: Exhibits *Navajos* in the *Summer Exhibition of Pictures* at the Salmagundi Club, New York

June–July: Holds an exhibition at the Stendahl Galleries, Ambassador Hotel, Los Angeles

Returns to the West Coast

Summer: Makes a sketching trip to New Mexico and Arizona

1931–1932 Fall–winter: In California; Evelyn still in school in New York

1932 March: Holds an exhibition at the Ebell Club, Los Angeles

April–June: Exhibits *Navajos* ($2,000) at the Los Angeles Museum of History, Science, and Art's *Painting and Sculpture Exhibition, Thirteenth Annual*

Spring: Evelyn graduates from high school

Spring: Payne has falling-out with gallery owner Earl Stendahl

June: Exhibits at the opening of the Ilsley Galleries, Ambassador Hotel, Los Angeles

July: The Stendahl Galleries, now located on Wilshire Boulevard (previously at the Ambassador Hotel, Los Angeles), uses nine Payne paintings to pay $5,300 in back rent to the Ambassador Hotel; paintings are *Sierra Krags* ($1,000), *Sierra Haze* ($600), *A Rugged Peak* ($500), *Mountain Pass* ($500), *Evening* ($500), *Making Ready* ($500), *A High Sierra Evening* ($500), *Heights of Kanderstag* ($600), and *A Riviera Village* ($600)

Summer: Payne makes his final Sierra trip with Elsie and Evelyn

Summer: Makes a sketching trip to New Mexico and Arizona

Edgar and Elsie Payne separate

1933 March 3–25: Exhibits *Packing In* in the *Annual Auction Sale* at the Salmagundi Club, New York

June: Payne's mother dies

Summer: Payne makes a sketching trip to New Mexico and Arizona

1934 March: Exhibits *Laguna Coast* and *Sierra Trail* under the auspices of the Public Works of Art Project, 14th Region—Southern California

June: Elsie opens the Payne-Kann Studio Gallery, Beverly Hills, with Marie H. Kann; dedicates the first show to Edgar Payne

Summer: Payne sketches and paints in the Sierra

Summer: Makes a sketching trip to New Mexico and Arizona

Fall: The Payne-Kann Studio Gallery becomes the Payne-Pegler Studio Gallery when Virginia Pegler replaces Marie Kann

November: Holds an exhibition at the Ilsley Galleries, Ambassador Hotel, Los Angeles

November–December: Holds an exhibition of forty-five small oils at the H. Taylor Brewitt Gallery, San Francisco

1935 January: Holds an exhibition at the Town House, Los Angeles

January: Exhibits *Fisherman's Harbor* at the Academy of Western Painters' *First Annual Exhibition*

February 9: Evelyn marries John Burton Hatcher at the Payne-Pegler Studio Gallery

1936 June: Payne exhibits in the *First Annual Salon of the Associated Artists and Patrons* at the Frances Webb Galleries, Los Angeles

September 14: After dissolution of the Payne-Pegler Studio Gallery, Elsie opens the Elsie Palmer Payne Art School and Gallery in Beverly Hills

Payne lives at 1142 North Seward Street, Hollywood

1939 Exhibits at the Golden Gate International Exposition, San Francisco

October 4: Southern California artists meet to form a Los Angeles branch of the Society for Sanity in Art; Payne becomes a charter member

1940 April: Included in the Society for Sanity in Art's first exhibition, held in Exposition Park, Los Angeles

April: Holds an exhibition at the Ebell Club, Los Angeles

1941 August: Payne painting is included in the Iowa Salon exhibition

Publishes the first edition of *Composition of Outdoor Painting* (Seward Publishing Company)

1944 March: Exhibits with twenty-eight members of the California Art Club at Bloomingdale's, New York

July: Exhibits *The Red Gorge* ($600) in *An Exhibition of Paintings and Sculptures by Fifty Members of the California Art Club,* Stendahl Art Galleries, Wilshire Boulevard, Los Angeles

October: Exhibits with the Glendale Art Association

1946 March 1: Payne's film, *Sierra Journey,* has its first showing at the Bell & Howell Auditorium, Los Angeles

Composition of Outdoor Painting goes into its second printing

Payne becomes ill with cancer; Elsie closes her Wilshire Boulevard studio and moves into his Hollywood home

1947 April: Payne exhibits *Temple Crags* at the Laguna Beach Art Association

April 8: Dies from cancer in Los Angeles

August: Memorial exhibition with William Wendt is held at the Laguna Beach Art Association

1948 February–March: Memorial exhibition is held at the Bowers Museum, Santa Ana

April: Payne's film, *Sierra Journey,* is shown at the California Art Club

April–May: Memorial exhibition is held in the art gallery of the Hollywood branch of the Los Angeles Public Library

April–May: The Riverside Art Association sponsors a memorial exhibition at the Riverside Public Library

June: Memorial exhibition is held at the Hollywood Athletic Club

1948–1949 November–January: Exhibition of Payne's work is held at the Ebell Club, Los Angeles

December–January: Exhibition of Payne's drawings is held at the Seward Street studio, Hollywood

1949 October: Exhibition is held in Thorne Hall, Occidental College, Los Angeles

Exhibition is held at Pomona College, Claremont, California

1952 April: Elsie Palmer Payne's bronze plaque of Payne is dedicated in the Edgar Alwin Payne room of the Laguna Beach Art Association

1954 September: Joint exhibition of Edgar and Elsie's work is held at the Glendale Public Library, Glendale, California

1955 September–November: Exhibition is held at the Mountain View Art Gallery, Altadena, California

1957 Elsie Palmer Payne obtains copyright for *Composition of Outdoor Painting,* which goes into its third printing

1958 Payne's gouaches are exhibited by the Laguna Beach Art Association

September–October: *Fifth Lake* is exhibited at the National Academy of Design's *Henry W. Ranger Centennial Exhibition*

1959 December: *Fifth Lake* is acquired by the Smithsonian Institution for the National Collection of Fine Arts and exhibited; it subsequently travels to museums in the southeastern United States

1963 Exhibition is held at the Panhandle-Plains Historical Museum, Canyon, Texas; the exhibition travels to the No Man's Land Historical Museum, Goodwell, Oklahoma

1965 March: Exhibition is held at the Bowman-Mann Gallery, Beverly Hills, California

1967 Works are exhibited at The American Artists Professional League

1968–1969 December–March: Exhibition of forty-four works, *The World of Edgar Payne,* is held at the Southeast Arkansas Arts and Science Center, Pine Bluff, Arkansas

1969 Elsie moves to Minneapolis with her daughter and son-in-law and founds Payne Studios Inc.

1970 April: Retrospective *Edgar Payne, 1882–1947: Western and Marine Paintings* is arranged by Denver artist Wolfgang Pogzeba and shown at the Kennedy Galleries, New York

1971 June 17: Elsie Palmer Payne dies

1973 October: Exhibition of nineteen paintings, *Edgar Alwin Payne, 1892 [sic]–1947: Memorial Exhibition,* is held at the Laguna Beach Museum of Art

1983 Exhibition is held at the Roberts Gallery, Pomona, California

1985 *Composition of Outdoor Painting* goes into its fourth printing

1987 Exhibition *Edgar Payne, 1882–1947* is held at the Goldfield Galleries, Los Angeles

1988 Rena Neumann Coen publishes *The Paynes, Edgar & Elsie: American Artists*

1997 March–April: Exhibition *Nature's Magnificence: Works by Edgar Payne (1883–1947)* is held at The Redfern Gallery, Laguna Beach

2000 November–December: Exhibition *Payne's Southwest* is held at Arizona West Galleries, Scottsdale, Arizona

2002 Evelyn Payne Hatcher publishes *The Drawings of Edgar Payne, 1883–1947*

2009 February 16: Evelyn Payne Hatcher dies

2012 February 11–May 6: Exhibition *Edgar Payne: The Scenic Journey* is held at the Crocker Art Museum, Sacramento, California

June 3–October 14: Exhibition *Edgar Payne: The Scenic Journey* is held at the Pasadena Museum of California Art, Pasadena

2012–2013 December 1–March 24: Exhibition *Edgar Payne: The Scenic Journey* is held at the Gilcrease Museum, Tulsa, Oklahoma

Edgar Payne's Ginger Jar with Pencils and Brushes, n.d. Ceramic, 5 x 4 x 4 in. Courtesy of DeRu's Fine Arts

SELECTED BIBLIOGRAPHY

Books and Exhibition Catalogues

Anderson, Antony, and Fred S. Hogue. *Edgar Alwin Payne and His Work*. Los Angeles: Stendahl Art Galleries, 1926.

Armfield, Maxwell. *An Artist in America*. London: Methuen, 1925.

Arnot Art Museum. *A Private Collection of Paintings by Some of the Living Artists of Southern California*. Elmira, NY: Arnot Art Museum, n.d.

Barron, Stephanie, Sheri Bernstein, and Ilene Susan Fort. *Made in California: Art, Image, and Identity, 1900–2000*. Los Angeles: Los Angeles County Museum of Art; Berkeley: University of California Press, 2000.

———, eds. *Reading California: Art, Image, and Identity, 1900–2000*. Los Angeles: Los Angeles County Museum of Art; Berkeley: University of California Press, 2000.

Brinton, Christian. *Illustrated Catalogue of the Post-Exposition Exhibition in the Department of Fine Arts, Panama-Pacific International Exposition*. San Francisco: San Francisco Art Association, 1915.

Bryce, James. *The American Commonwealth*. 2 vols. New York: Macmillan, 1912.

Coen, Rena Neumann. *Elsie Palmer Payne: Out of the Shadow; A Retrospective Exhibition*. Minneapolis, MN: Payne Studios, 1988.

———. *The Paynes, Edgar & Elsie: American Artists*. Minneapolis, MN: Payne Studios, 1988.

Corn, Wanda. *The Color of Mood: American Tonalism, 1880–1910*. San Francisco: M. H. de Young Memorial Museum and California Palace of the Legion of Honor, 1972.

Emerson, Ralph Waldo, and Henry David Thoreau. *Nature/Walking*. With an introduction by John Elder. Boston: Beacon Press, 1991.

Enman, Tom K. *Edgar Alwin Payne, 1892 [sic]–1947: Memorial Exhibition*. Laguna Beach, CA: Laguna Beach Museum of Art, c. 1973.

Falk, Peter H., and Andrea Ansell Bien, eds. *The Annual Exhibition Record of the Art Institute of Chicago, 1888–1950*. Madison, CT: Sound View Press, 1990.

———. *The Annual Exhibition Record of the National Academy of Design, 1901–1950: Incorporating the Annual Exhibitions, 1901–1950, and the Winter Exhibitions, 1906–1932*. Madison, CT: Sound View Press, 1990.

Falk, Peter H., and Anna Wells Rutledge, eds. *The Annual Exhibition Record of the Pennsylvania Academy of the Fine Arts*. Madison, CT: Sound View Press, 1988–1989.

Gerdts, William H., and Will South. *California Impressionism*. New York: Abbeville Press, 1998.

Gillihan, James E. *The World of Edgar Payne*. Pine Bluff, AR: Southeast Arkansas Arts and Science Center, 1969.

Goldfield Galleries. *Edgar Payne (1882–1947)*. With an introduction by Edward Goldfield and a biography by Nancy Moure. Los Angeles: Goldfield Galleries, 1987.

Harry Linder Studios. *Exhibition of Paintings by Edgar Payne*. Long Beach, CA: Harry Linder Studios, n.d.

Hatcher, Evelyn Payne. *The Drawings of Edgar Payne, 1883–1947*. With an introduction by Jean Stern. Minneapolis, MN: Payne Studios, 2002.

Hays, A. P. *Payne's Southwest*. Scottsdale, AZ: Arizona West Galleries, 2000.

Hicks, Jack, James D. Houston, Maxine Hong Kingston, and Al Young, eds. *The Literature of California: Writings from the Golden State*. Vol 1. Berkeley: University of California Press, 2000.

Hogue, Fred. *Exhibition of Contemporary American Art: "Salon of Art."* Los Angeles: Ebell Club, 1930.

Hough, Katherine Plake, Michael R. Grauer, and Helen Laird. *Carl Oscar Borg: A Niche in Time; Essays by Katherine Plake Hough, Michael R. Grauer, and Helen Laird*. Palm Springs, CA: Palm Springs Desert Museum, 1990.

Hughes, Edan Milton. *Artists in California, 1786–1940*. 3rd ed. 2 vols. Sacramento, CA: Crocker Art Museum, 2002.

Huntington, David C. "The Quest for Unity: American Art Between the World's Fairs, 1876–1893." In *The Quest for Unity: American Art Between the World's Fairs, 1876–1893*. Detroit: Detroit Institute of Arts, 1983.

James, George Wharton. *California, Romantic and Beautiful*. Boston: Page Company, 1914.

Opposite: *Sycamore in Autumn, Orange County Park* (detail, p. 30), c. 1917

Jeffers, Robinson. *Roan Stallion, Tamar, and Other Poems*. New York: Peter G. Boyle, 1924. Reprint, New York: Boni & Liveright, 1925.

Kennedy Galleries. *Edgar Payne, 1882–1947: An Exhibition of Western and Marine Painting*. New York: Kennedy Galleries, 1970.

Longstreth, Richard. *On the Edge of the World: Four Architects in San Francisco at the Turn of the Century*. New York: Architectural History Foundation; Cambridge, MA: MIT Press, 1983.

Markham, Edwin. *California the Wonderful: Her Romantic History, Her Picturesque People, Her Wild Shores, Her Desert Mystery, Her Valley Loveliness, Her Mountain Glory, Including Her Varied Resources, Her Commercial Greatness, Her Intellectual Achievements, Her Expanding Hopes, with Glimpses of Oregon and Washington, Her Northern Neighbors*. New York: Hearst's International Library, 1914.

McGinnis, John, ed. *Changing Times / Changing Styles: The Ruth Stoever Fleming Collection of Southern California Art*. Newport Beach and Costa Mesa, CA: Newport-Mesa Unified School District, 1985.

Midland Club. *Exhibition of Paintings by Edgar Alwin Payne in the Lounge of [the] Midland Club*. Chicago: Midland Club, May 1931.

Mountain View Art Gallery. *Edgar Alwin Payne*. Altadena, CA: Mountain View Art Gallery, 1955.

Moure, Nancy Dustin Wall. *Artists' Clubs and Exhibitions in Los Angeles Before 1930*. Publications in Southern California Art, no. 2. Los Angeles: Privately printed, 1974.

———. *California Art: 450 Years of Painting and Other Media*. Los Angeles: Dustin Publications, 1998.

———. *Dictionary of Art and Artists in Southern California Before 1930*. With an introduction by Carl Schaefer Dentzel. Publications in Southern California Art, no. 3. Glendale, CA: Dustin Publications, 1975.

Muir, John. *The Yosemite*. New York: Century, 1912. Reprint, Garden City, NY: Doubleday, 1962.

Muirhead, Findlay, ed. *Muirhead's Switzerland: A Guide Book of Switzerland, with the Chamonix and the Italian Lakes*. New York: Macmillan, 1923.

Nash, Roderick, ed. *The Call of the Wild: 1900–1916*. New York: George Braziller, 1970.

Neff, Emily Ballew, and Barry Lopez. *The Modern West: American Landscapes, 1890–1950*. New Haven, CT: Yale University Press; Houston, TX: Museum of Fine Arts, Houston, 2006.

Occidental College Art Department. *Edgar Alwin Payne*. Los Angeles: Occidental College Art Department, 1949.

Payne, Edgar A. *Composition of Outdoor Painting*. Hollywood, CA: Seward, 1941. Reprint, 7th ed., edited by DeRu's Fine Arts with addenda by Evelyn Payne Hatcher, Bellflower, CA: DeRu's Fine Arts, 2005.

Porter, Bruce, Everett Maxwell, Porter Garnett, Hector Alliot, Michael Williams, Antony Anderson, Alma May Cook, Willis Polk, John E. D. Trask, A. B. Clark, John McLure Hamilton, John I. Walter, Robert B. Harshe, Mabel Urmy Seares, Pedro J. Lemos, Hill Tolerton, Hamilton Wright, John McLaren, A. Stirling Calder, Louis Christian Mullgardt, and Bernard R. Maybeck. *Art in California: A Survey of American Art with Special Reference to Californian Painting, Sculpture, and Architecture Past and Present, Particularly as Those Arts Were Represented at the Panama-Pacific International Exposition*. San Francisco: R. L. Bernier, 1916. Reprint, Irvine, CA: Westphal, 1988.

Poulton, Donna L., and Vern G. Swanson. *Painters of Utah's Canyons and Deserts*. With a foreword by Donald J. Hagerty. Layton, UT: Gibbs Smith, 2009.

Powers, Willow Roberts. *Navajo Trading: The End of an Era*. Albuquerque: University of New Mexico Press, 2001.

Redfern Gallery. *Nature's Magnificence: Works by Edgar Payne (1883–1947)*. Laguna Beach, CA: Redfern Gallery, 1997.

Roosevelt, Theodore. "Nationalism in Literature and Art." In *The Works of Theodore Roosevelt*. National ed. Vol. 12, 325–336. New York: Scribner's Sons, 1926.

Ruskin, John. *Selections from the Writings of John Ruskin*. New York: John Wiley and Sons, 1868.

Smyth, H. Warington. *Mast and Sail in Europe and Asia*, 231–286. London: John Murray, 1906.

Stendahl Art Galleries. *An Exhibition of Paintings and Sculptures by Fifty Members of The California Art Club*. Los Angeles: Stendahl Art Galleries, 1944.

Stern, Jean, and Janet Dominik. *Masterworks of California Impressionism: The FFCA, Morton H. Fleischer Collection*. 2nd ed. Phoenix, AZ: Franchise Finance Corporation of America, 1986.

Stern, Jean, and William H. Gerdts. *Masters of Light: Plein-Air Painting in California, 1890–1930*. Irvine, CA: The Irvine Museum, 2002.

Stoddard, John L. "Switzerland." In *Norway, Switzerland, Athens, Venice*. Vol. 1 of *John L. Stoddard's Lectures*. Chicago: Shuman, 1912.

Taft, Robert. *Artists and Illustrators of the Old West, 1850–1900*. New York: Scribner's Sons, 1953.

Thoreau, Henry David. "Walden." In *Great Short Works of Henry David Thoreau*, edited by Wendell Glick. New York: HarperPerennial, 1993.

Trenton, Patricia, and William H. Gerdts, eds. *California Light, 1900–1930*. Laguna Beach, CA: Laguna Art Museum, 1990.

Westphal, Ruth Lilly, ed. *Plein Air Painters of California: The Southland*. Irvine, CA: Westphal, 1982.

Wyatt, David. *The Fall into Eden: Landscape and Imagination in California*. Cambridge: Cambridge University Press, 1986. Reprint, 1988.

Periodicals, Newspapers, and Unpublished Sources

Anderson, Antony. Art and Artists. *Los Angeles Times*, August 19, 1906; September 3, 1911; September 17, 1911.

———. "Edgar Payne, Painter and World Traveler." *Laguna Beach South Coast News*, June 21, 1929.

———. "Fresh Breeze from Laguna." *Los Angeles Times*, July 7, 1929.

———. In the Realm of Art. *Los Angeles Times*, November 17, 1918, and March 9, 1919.

———. "Laguna Art Notes." *Los Angeles Times*, June 10, 1928.

———. "Laguna Exhibition." *Los Angeles Times*, March 25, 1928.

———. Of Art and Artists. *Los Angeles Times*, April 8, 1917; August 10, 1919; September 28, 1919; February 1, 1920; June 13, 1920; December 19, 1920; January 30, 1921; February 20, 1921; November 20, 1921; February 12, 1922; May 28, 1922; July 2, 1922; November 5, 1922; November 12, 1922; April 22, 1923; April 29, 1923; July 15, 1923; December 30, 1923; March 9, 1924; April 6, 1924; November 16, 1924; March 29, 1925; April 26, 1925; May 10, 1925.

———. "Popular Prizes at Laguna." *Los Angeles Times*, September 2, 1928.

[———]. "Some Newsy Notes on Matters of Art." *Los Angeles Times*, May 31, 1925.

Arbellot, Simon. "Un petit incident aux artistes français." *Le Figaro* (Paris), May 3, 1924.

"Art and Artists." Newspaper clipping. Edgar and Elsie Palmer Payne Papers. DeRu's Fine Arts, Bellflower, CA.

"Art in Chicago." *Art and Progress* 5 (October 1914): 439–440.

"Art News of Near-By Cities: Genius Near Home." *Artland*, August 1926, 30–31.

"Bartlett Galleries." *California Art and Artists* 35–36 (July 1929): 57.

Bennett, Charles A. "Edgar Payne's Beautiful Painting." *Peoria Journal*, May 31, 1914.

Berkeley (CA) Gazette. "Paintings Secured for Private Collections." February 19, 1927.

Biermann, Daisy Kessler. "Spirit of California Idealized in Exhibit of Well-Known Chicago Artist Who Has Transferred Tourmaline Glow to Canvas." Newspaper clipping, 1921. Edgar and Elsie Palmer Payne Papers. DeRu's Fine Arts, Bellflower, CA.

Bingham, Elizabeth. Art. *Saturday Night*, May 28, 1927.

———. Art Exhibits and Comment. *Saturday Night*, February 11, 1922; June 10, 1922.

Bishoff, Murray. "Artist with Barry County Roots Gains Notoriety." *Monett (MO) Times*, May 12, 2009.

Brown, Vandyke [Antony Anderson]. "Los Angeles Letter." *Life and Art* 9 (June 2, 1922).

"California Art Club President Exhibits." *California Graphic*, May 29, 1926.

Chicago Evening Post. May 10, 1913.

———. "Art World." December 16, 1924.

———. "At Newcomb & Macklin's." "Magazine of the Art World," supplement. April 7, 1925.

———. "Edgar Payne's Paintings." November 10, 1925.

———. "'Snow-Clad Heights'—Edgar Alwin Payne." December 16, 1924.

Chicago Daily Tribune. "Payne Art Pleasing and Intelligible." June 27, 1914.

C., H. S. "Paris." *Art News* 22 (April 12, 1924): 9.

"Colorful Vessels . . . and Alpine Crags." Newspaper clipping, 1926. Edgar and Elsie Palmer Payne Papers. DeRu's Fine Arts, Bellflower, CA.

Cook, Alma May. "Close Contact Provides Understanding for True Career." *Los Angeles Express,* June 2, 1926.

———. "Edgar Payne to Tour in Europe." *Los Angeles Express,* May 22, 1922.

———. "Los Angeles to See New Payne Exhibit." *Los Angeles Express,* 1932. Newspaper clipping, Edgar and Elsie Palmer Payne Papers. DeRu's Fine Arts, Bellflower, CA.

Cox-McCormack, Nancy, and Lawrence S. Rainey. "Ezra Pound in the Paris Years." *Sewanee Review* 102 (Winter 1994): 93–95.

D., F. "Two Brilliant Artists Show in Paris Mansion." *Paris— Evening Telegraph,* March 28, 1924.

"Edgar Alwin Payne." *California Southland,* July 1927, 6.

"Edgar Alwin Payne." *Southland Artist* 2 (October 1965): 30–31.

"Edgar Alwin Payne Has New Showing in Galleries." *Allerton House Magazine,* May 1929, 6.

"Edgar Alwyn [sic] Payne." *California Art and Artists* 35–36 (October 1929): 63.

Edgar and Elsie Palmer Payne Papers. DeRu's Fine Arts, Bellflower, CA.

"Edgar A. Payne, Noted Painter, Writer, Uses Schmincke Finest Artists' Oil Colors." Advertisement. *Art Digest,* September 1, 1941.

"Edgar Payne." *Artland* 1 (May 29, 1926): 5.

"Edgar Payne." *California Art and Artists* 35–36 (July 1929): 58.

"Edgar Payne." *California Art and Artists* 39–40 (July 1931): 9–10.

"Few Americans in the Rome Biennial." *Art News* 22 (December 15, 1923): 5.

Gaut, Helen Lukens. "Motoring in Southern California." *Craftsman* 22 (August 1912): 510–517.

Glendale (CA) News. "Talks to P.T.A. on Furnishings." March 9, 1924.

"Great Art Exhibit Will Be Shown in Col. James' Room." Newspaper clipping, May 1948. Edgar and Elsie Palmer Payne Papers. DeRu's Fine Arts, Bellflower, CA.

Heitkamp, Ernest L. "Art and Artists: Payne Is Great Painter." *Chicago Herald,* July 17, 1927.

———. "Refinement of His Art Makes Payne a Great Painter, Says Heitkamp." *Chicago Herald and Examiner,* July 17, 1927.

Henry, H. Raymond. "Painter's Work on Behalf of the Southland Art Told By Writer." Newspaper clipping. Ferdinand Perrett Papers. Archives of American Art, Smithsonian Institution, Washington, DC. Reel no. 3862, frame 50.

Hills, Anna A. "The Laguna Beach Art Association." *American Magazine of Art* 10 (October 1919): 459–463.

Hogue, Fred. "The God of the Mountains." *Los Angeles Times,* May 22, 1927.

———. "Grandeur of California Sierras: Paints Sunset Glow and Morning Light." *Hemet (CA) News,* July 1, 1927.

Hogue, S. Fred. "The Art of Edgar Alwyn [sic] Payne." *Los Angeles Times,* May 23, 1926.

Hollywood Citizen-News. "Art and Artists: Smithsonian Likes Payne Painting." May 15, 1959.

———. "At Little Gallery." May 14, 1932.

———. "Edgar O. [sic] Payne, Landscapist, Answers Call." April 8, 1947.

Jewett, Eleanor. "First Shows of the Season Rival the Earlier Offerings in Their Worth and Colorfulness." *Chicago Daily Tribune,* May 25, 1930.

———. "Galleries Present New Exhibits." *Chicago Daily Tribune,* May 25, 1930.

Laguna Beach Life. "Edgar A. Payne Opens One-Man Show on 15th at Stendahl Gallery." May 14, 1926.

———. "Miss Ann Mason Entertains for Laguna Artist." July 2, 1925.

———. "Payne Receives Merited Recognition." August 10, 1923.

Laguna Beach South Coast News, February 15, 1929.

———. "Gallery Exhibits Are Memorials to Payne, Wendt." Newspaper clipping. Edgar and Elsie Palmer Payne Papers. DeRu's Fine Arts, Bellflower, CA.

———. "Memorial Show of Payne, Wendt Art Nears End." August 20, 1947.

———. "Payne Film, Sale Set for Gallery Next Saturday." Newspaper clipping. Edgar and Elsie Palmer Payne Papers. DeRu's Fine Arts, Bellflower, CA.

La revue moderne illustrée des arts et de la vie. "Les expositions particulières: Mme Nancy Cox McCormack et M. Edgar Alwin Payne à Hôtel Seligmann." May 15, 1924.

Lewis, Lloyd D. "Vigorous Art Shown at Palette and Chisel Club." Newspaper clipping, 1916. Edgar and Elsie Palmer Payne Papers. DeRu's Fine Arts, Bellflower, CA.

Los Angeles Express. "Landscape Artist Has Hobby of Building Ship Replicas: Tiny Models on Display in Ambassador Hotel Lobby." June 18, 1926.

Los Angeles Times, June 16, 1929.

Los Angeles Times, October 23, 1921.

———. "Arizona State Fair Opens November 12." October 28, 1928.

———. "Art Exhibitions Reviewed." July 12, 1936.

———. "Art Exhibits in Southland." July 29, 1928.

———. "Current Art Exhibitions." June 2, 1929.

———. "East Likes Southland Art." October 20, 1929.

———. "Edgar Payne at the Cannell Gallery." December 23, 1923.

———. "Edgar Payne Sees the Italian Peaks." April 29, 1923.

———. "Exhibit of Oils Arranged Here." December 16, 1928.

———. "Exhibits Briefly Reviewed." September 8, 1929.

———. "Fine Display at Laguna Exhibit." April 7, 1929.

———. "From Boats to Surrealism." March 27, 1932.

———. "Gen. Gourand Meets with Edgar Payne." August 7, 1923.

———. "Gossip from Studios." August 19, 1928.

———. "Laguna Beach School to Add to Art Gallery." October 16, 1926.

———. "News from Laguna Beach." February 20, 1921.

———. "News of the Art World." May 5, 1929.

———. "Of Interest to Artists." December 16, 1923.

———. "On Painting for 'The People.'" August 5, 1928.

———. "Painters Give Work to School." November 22, 1926.

———. "Pointers for Painters." August 31, 1941.

———. "Southland Has Honors at Fair." August 23, 1926.

———. "Stuber and Payne." January 22, 1928.

———. "Studies in the Decorative." August 7, 1927.

———. "Tribute Paid Noted Artist." May 23, 1922.

———. "Twelve Masters at Pasadena." August 26, 1928.

———. "Twelve Pictures Are Just Enough." December 28, 1924.

———. "Western Art on View." December 8, 1929.

Marquis, Neeta. "Artist Back After Absence: Pictures Placed on Exhibition." *Los Angeles Times,* June 23, 1929.

———. "Southland Artist Holds Paris Exhibit." *Los Angeles Times,* November 22, 1925.

Marsh, Mary. "Art." *Los Angeles Times,* May 29, 1926.

Martin, Lannie Haynes. Article for Arthur Millier column Art and Artists. *Los Angeles Times,* August 5, 1928.

Maxwell, Everett C. "Exhibition of California Art Club." *Fine Arts Journal* 28 (January–June 1913): 189.

McCauley, Lena M. "Mountains and Sea in Payne's Exhibit." "Magazine of the Art World," supplement. *Chicago Evening Post,* June 21, 1927.

McFetridge, W. H. "Art Notes." *San Diego Tribune,* 1920. Newspaper clipping, Edgar and Elsie Palmer Payne Papers. DeRu's Fine Arts, Bellflower, CA.

Merrell, Eric. "A Visit with Evelyn Payne Hatcher, Daughter of Edgar and Elsie Payne." *California Art Club Newsletter,* June 2001, 1–5.

Millier, Arthur. Art and Artists. *Los Angeles Times,* May 22, 1927; August 7, 1927; August 5, 1928; November 11, 1928; June 16, 1929.

———. Of Art and Artists. *Los Angeles Times,* May 23, 1926.

———. "Our Artists in Person." *Los Angeles Times,* July 5, 1931.

Miner, Frederick Roland. "California: The Landscapist's Land of Heart's Desire." *Western Art* 1 (June–August 1914): 31–34.

Montgelas, Albrecht. "Payne Shows Realism on Canvas." Newspaper clipping, 1916. Edgar and Elsie Palmer Payne Papers. DeRu's Fine Arts, Bellflower, CA.

"The New Art Gallery in Laguna." *Critique* 1 (Spring 1929): 21.

New York Herald, Paris edition. "Rome Art Show Draws Society: Name of Members of American Colony and Visitors to the Eternal City." Newspaper clipping, 1924. Edgar and Elsie Palmer Payne Papers. DeRu's Fine Arts, Bellflower, CA.

——. "Two Well-Known American Artists Exhibit Bronzes and Paintings." March 16, 1924.

New York Times. "Americans Shine in Paris Salon." May 1, 1923.

——. "America to Send Art Exhibit to Rome." July 15, 1923.

——. "Contemporary Art Placed on Display." March 9, 1944.

——. "Edgar Alwin Payne: Artist Was Known for Paintings of Alps and Sierras." April 9, 1947.

——. "J. Seligmann Dies: Noted Art Dealer." November 1, 1923.

——. "Paris Salon Stirs Trouble with Artists: Groups Foreign Exhibitors by Themselves—Frenchmen Join in Protest." April 30, 1924.

——. "Rome to See Our Art." November 18, 1923.

Norris, Frank. "The Frontier Gone at Last." *World's Work* 3 (1902): 1728–1731.

"Notable Exhibition at Orr Galleries." Newspaper clipping. Edgar and Elsie Palmer Payne Papers. DeRu's Fine Arts, Bellflower, CA.

"Open Art Gallery at Laguna Beach Tomorrow P.M." Newspaper clipping, July 26, 1918. Edgar and Elsie Palmer Payne Papers. DeRu's Fine Arts, Bellflower, CA.

Ozzie. "Laguna Art Colony Known in Far Distant Cities." *Laguna Beach South Coast News,* July 9, 1943.

"Paintings by Edgar Payne on View." Newspaper clipping. Edgar and Elsie Palmer Payne Papers. DeRu's Fine Arts, Bellflower, CA.

Pallen, Agnes Elding. "Artist Celebrities Find Ideal Homes in California: Famous Painters of World Get Inspiration for Work amid Southland's Romance." *Los Angeles Times,* January 17, 1926.

Payne, Edgar A. "Bolshevik Control Seen in 'New' Art: Noted Artist Flays 'Red' Influence in Expression." Newspaper clipping. Edgar and Elsie Palmer Payne Papers. DeRu's Fine Arts, Bellflower, CA.

——. "In Switzerland: A Letter Dated 15 de Avril." *Laguna Beach Life,* May 18, 1923.

——. "World Peace." Undated, unpublished typescript. Edgar and Elsie Palmer Payne Papers. DeRu's Fine Arts, Bellflower, CA.

Payne, Elsie Palmer. "Edgar Payne: Biographical Notes." Undated, unpublished typescript. Edgar and Elsie Palmer Payne Papers. DeRu's Fine Arts, Bellflower, CA.

——. *A Tribute to Edgar Alwin Payne.* Los Angeles, n.d.

Pennell, Elizabeth Robins. "Venetian Boats." *Harper's New Monthly Magazine* 80 (March 1890): 554–555.

Peoria Journal. Newspaper clipping, March 26, 1916. Edgar and Elsie Palmer Payne Papers. DeRu's Fine Arts, Bellflower, CA.

——. Newspaper clipping, 1917. Edgar and Elsie Palmer Payne Papers. DeRu's Fine Arts, Bellflower, CA.

Petersen, Martin E. "Edgar Payne." *Artists of the Rockies and the Golden West* 6 (Summer 1979): 52–57.

Pierce, Mary Anne. "Priceless Painting Hangs in Courthouse." *Terre Haute (IN) Tribune-Star.* Newspaper clipping, Edgar and Elsie Palmer Payne Papers. DeRu's Fine Arts, Bellflower, CA.

"Plaque to Honor Laguna Artist." Newspaper clipping, April 3, 1952. Edgar and Elsie Palmer Payne Papers. DeRu's Fine Arts, Bellflower, CA.

Powers, Laura Bride. "Art and Artists Around the Bay." *Oakland Tribune,* June 1916. Newspaper clipping. Archives of the Oakland Museum of California.

Russell, John. "Germain Seligman, Dealer and Expert in French Art." *New York Times,* March 28, 1978.

Salt Lake Tribune. "Chicago Artist of Note Offers Show at Ogden." Newspaper clipping, 1929. Edgar and Elsie Palmer Payne Papers. DeRu's Fine Arts, Bellflower, CA.

——. "Payne Canvases Suggest Term, Poems of Color." July 13, 1930.

——. "Wilderness of High Sierras Presents Lure for Artist." July 29, 1928.

San Diego Sun. "California on Canvas." April 6, 1921.

San Diego Tribune. "Art Notes." April 9, 1921.

Santa Ana Daily Register. "Edgar Payne Picture Wins Kahn Prize at Chicago Institute." December 3, 1920.

——. "Laguna Artist to Exhibit Pictures." March 15, 1923.

Sawyer, Phil. "In Color and Clay." *Chicago Daily Tribune,* 1924. Newspaper clipping. Edgar and Elsie Palmer Payne Papers. DeRu's Fine Arts, Bellflower, CA.

Schad, Jasper G. "'A City of Picture Buyers': Art, Identity, and Aspiration in Los Angeles and Southern California, 1891–1914." *Southern California Quarterly* 92 (Spring 2010): 19–50.

St. Clair, Gordon. "The Edgar Payne Exhibition." Clipping from the *Inland Printer*. Edgar and Elsie Palmer Payne Papers. DeRu's Fine Arts, Bellflower, CA.

———. "Edgar Payne Is Tremendous Worker at Chosen Vocation." Newspaper clipping. Edgar and Elsie Palmer Payne Papers. DeRu's Fine Arts, Bellflower, CA.

———. "Edgar Payne's California Paintings." *Inland Stationer,* 1915, 160.

Stendahl Art Gallery Records. Archives of American Art, Smithsonian Institution, Washington, DC. Reels no. 2716, 2717.

Stickley, Gustav. "Nature and Art in California." *Craftsman* 6 (July 1904): 370–390.

Vickerman, Tom. "Payne Paintings at Allerton Club." *Chicago Evening Post,* May 14, 1929.

Wakefield, Paul. "Texas Boy, Once a 'Sign Dauber,' Becomes a Famous Painter in Oil." *Laguna Beach South Coast News,* March 12, 1916.

Walker, Caroline. "Art Exhibition Vivifies Cal. Mountains." Newspaper clipping, 1926. Edgar and Elsie Palmer Payne Papers. DeRu's Fine Arts, Bellflower, CA.

Walter, Paul A. F. "The Santa Fe–Taos Art Movement." *Art and Archaeology* 4 (December 1916): 330–338.

Williams, Michael. "A Pageant of American Art." *Art and Progress* 6 (August 1915): 337–353.

Winchell, Anna Cora. Artists and Their Work. *San Francisco Chronicle,* December 15, 1918; April 27, 1919; September 21, 1919.

Wolfson, Sonia. "Art and Artists: Payne and Gilbert at Stendahl's." *California Graphic,* May 28, 1927.

Flowers [Ranunculus], 1937. Oil on canvas on board, 16 x 20 in. Private collection. Courtesy of DeRu's Fine Arts

EXHIBITION CHECKLIST

Adriatic Cargo Boats, Chioggia, Italy, c. 1923
Oil on canvas, 42½ x 42½ in.
Collection of D. L. Stuart Jr.
(p. 128)

Along the Riviera, Menton, France, 1922
Oil on canvas, 29 x 29 in.
Collection of James Taylor and Gary Conway
(p. 119)

Alpine Village—Switzerland, c. 1922
Oil on canvas, 42 x 42 in.
Weinstein Family Trust
(pp. 110–111)

Arched Trees, n.d.
Pencil on paper, 8 x 10 in.
Collection of Mr. and Mrs. Jon R. Stuart
(p. 26)

Arizona Clouds, n.d.
Oil on canvas, 28 x 34 in.
Collection of Paul and Kathleen Bagley
(p. 16)

The Bay of Avalon, 1911
Oil on canvas, 33 x 42 in.
The Edward H. and Yvonne J. Boseker Collection
(p. 53)

Blue Canyon, after 1929
Oil on canvas, 34 x 34 in.
Private collection
(p. 210)

Breton Fishermen Unloading Fish, c. 1928
Photograph
Courtesy of DeRu's Fine Arts
(p. 148)

Breton Tuna Boats, Concarneau, France, c. 1924
Oil on canvas, 40 x 50 in.
Private collection
(pp. 164–165)

Brittany Boats, c. 1924
Oil on canvas, 28 x 34 in.
Private collection
(p. 160)

Brittany Boats, c. 1924
Oil on canvas, 30 x 40 in.
Robert and Nadine Hall Collection
(p. 108 [detail], p. 158)

Brittany Boats, c. 1924
Oil on canvas, 40 x 50 in.
Collection of D. L. Stuart Jr.
(p. 159)

Brittany Harbor, c. 1924
Oil on canvas, 28 x 34 in.
Courtesy of Redfern Gallery
(pp. 156–157)

Burning the Hogan, c. 1930s
Oil on canvas, 28 x 34 in.
Courtesy of Arizona West Galleries
(p. 206)

Canyon de Chelly, n.d.
Oil on canvas, 28 x 34 in.
Private collection
(p. 188)

Canyon de Chelly, n.d.
Oil on canvas, 28 x 34 in.
Courtesy of the Springville Museum of Art,
Springville, Utah
(pp. 216–217)

Canyon de Chelly, 1916
Oil on canvas, 27½ x 33¼ in.
Courtesy of the National Park Service, Hubbell
Trading Post National Historic Site, HUTR 5279
(p. 192)

Canyon Mission Viejo, Capistrano, n.d.
Oil on canvas, 24 x 28 in.
Private collection
Courtesy of The Irvine Museum
(p. 52)

Canyon Riders, n.d.
Oil on canvas, 25 x 30 in.
Collection of Reed and Chris Halladay
(p. 27 [detail], p. 184)

Capistrano Canyon, n.d.
Oil on canvas, 24 x 28 in.
Private collection
Courtesy of The Irvine Museum
(p. 29)

Capistrano Canyon, n.d.
Oil on canvas, 28 x 34 in.
Private collection
Courtesy of The Irvine Museum
(p. 20 [detail], p. 41)

Cargo Boats, Chioggia, Italy, 1923
Oil on canvas, 43 x 43 in.
The Buck Collection, Laguna Beach, California
(p. 129)

Carved frame for *When the Tide Is Low, Laguna Beach*, n.d.
Wood, 12 x 16 in.
Collection of Simon K. Chiu
(p. 87)

Château de Montrésor [Loire Valley, France], c. 1924
Oil on canvas, 29 x 29 in.
Collection of Betty Goldfield
(p. 146)

Château on the Way to Brittany, n.d.
Pencil on paper, 10 x 10 in.
Courtesy of DeRu's Fine Arts
(p. 147)

Chioggia Boats, n.d.
Photograph
Courtesy of DeRu's Fine Arts
(p. 124)

Chioggia Boats at Home [Italy], n.d.
Pencil on paper, 10 x 12 in.
Collection of Ruth and Robert Mirvis
(p. 126)

Composition Study for Navajo Horsemen, after 1929
Pencil on paper, 12 x 17 in.
Collection of Ruth and Robert Mirvis
(p. 200)

Desert Cloud Study, n.d.
Pencil on paper, 8 x 10 in.
Courtesy of DeRu's Fine Arts
(not shown)

Edgar Payne's Ginger Jar with Pencils and Brushes, n.d.
Ceramic, 5 x 4 x 4 in.
Courtesy of DeRu's Fine Arts
(p. 241)

Eternal Surge, c. 1920
Oil on canvas, 34 x 54 in.
Laguna Art Museum Collection
Museum Purchase with funds from prior gift
of Louis Outerbridge, 2002.009
(p. 63)

Eucalypti, n.d.
Pencil on paper, 11 x 8½ in.
Collection of Mr. and Mrs. Jon R. Stuart
(p. 48)

Fifth Lake [High Sierra], c. 1928
Oil on canvas, 40⅜ x 50¼ in.
Smithsonian American Art Museum, Washington, DC
Bequest of Henry Ward Ranger through the National
Academy of Design, 1957.10.6
(p. 92)

Fishermen's Wives Bargaining, Breton Scene, Concarneau, 1924
Oil on canvas, 32 x 42 in.
Payton Family Collection
(pp. 150–151)

Flowers [Ranunculus], 1937
Oil on canvas on board, 16 x 20 in.
Private collection
Courtesy of DeRu's Fine Arts
(p. 250)

The Grand Canyon, n.d.
Pencil on paper, 8 x 10½ in.
Collection of Mr. and Mrs. Jon R. Stuart
(p. 215)

Le Grand Pic Blanc, 1922
Oil on canvas, 43 x 43 in.
The Ruth Stoever-Fleming Collection of
Southern California Art
(p. 116)

Granite Slopes, 1920–1921
Oil on canvas, 34 x 34 in.
Private collection
Courtesy of George Stern Fine Arts
(p. 38)

The Great White Peak [Mt. Blanc, France], 1924
Oil on canvas, 62 x 62 in.
Los Angeles County Museum of Art
Gift of James N. and Linda S. Ries in memory of
Harold and Dorothy Shrier, M.2000.181
(p. 145)

Les Haut Sierra [High Sierra], c. 1922
Oil on canvas, 43 x 43 in.
Courtesy of Redfern Gallery
(p. 88)

Hexagonal Table, n.d.
Wood, 32 x 30 x 30 in.
Courtesy of DeRu's Fine Arts
(p. 15)

Hills in California, n.d.
Pencil on paper, 8 x 10 in.
Courtesy of DeRu's Fine Arts
(p. 35)

Hills of Altadena, 1917–1919
Oil on canvas, 36 x 45 in.
Steven Stern Collection
(p. 28)

The Homeport, Concarneau, c. 1924
Oil on canvas, 28 x 34 in.
Collection of Paul and Kathleen Bagley
(p. 167)

Idea Drawing for a Wood Sculpture, c. 1925
Pencil on paper, 11 x 9 in.
Courtesy of DeRu's Fine Arts
(p. 14)

Indians in Canyon, n.d.
Pencil on paper, 8 x 10 in.
Collection of Ruth and Robert Mirvis
(not shown)

In the Canal, Chioggia, c. 1923
Oil on canvas, 28 x 34 in.
Courtesy of William A. Karges Fine Art
(p. 168)

Italian Boats at Harbor, c. 1923
Oil on canvas, 28 x 34 in.
Payton Family Collection
(p. 169)

Italian Cargo Boat, Chioggia, Italy, n.d.
Photograph
Courtesy of DeRu's Fine Arts
(p. 124)

The Jungfrau, 1923–1924
Oil on canvas, 62 x 62 in.
Collection of Paul and Kathleen Bagley
(p. 138)

Pack Train in the High Sierra, 1930s
Oil on canvas, 30 x 40 in.
Collection of Gilbert and Nancy Waldman
Courtesy of John R. Howard Fine Art
(p. 76)

Painted place cards: *Crashing Surf, Meadow, High Sierra,*
presented to guests at banquet dinner hosted by the
Stendahl Galleries, May 22, 1922
Oil on board, each 2¼ x 3¾ in.
Collection of Jean and Linda Stern
(p. 86)

Profile View of Seated Navajo, n.d.
Photograph
Courtesy of DeRu's Fine Arts
(p. 12)

The Race, 1922
Oil on canvas, 28 x 34 in.
Private collection
Courtesy of Trotter Galleries
(p. 161)

Red Mesa, Monument Valley, Utah, c. 1935
Oil on canvas, 25 x 30 in.
Utah Museum of Fine Arts, University of Utah,
Salt Lake City, Utah
Purchased with funds from the Phyllis Canon Wattis
Endowment for Modern and Contemporary Art,
and Diane and Sam Stewart
(p. 176 [detail], p. 212)

The Rendezvous (Santa Cruz Island, CA), 1915
Oil on canvas, 33 x 42 in.
Private collection
(frontispiece [detail], pp. 54–55)

Restless Sea, 1917
Oil on canvas, 43 x 51 in.
Indianapolis Museum of Art
Gift of Mrs. James Sweetser, 17.66
(p. 60)

Rugged Slopes and Tamarack, c. 1919
Oil on board, 45 x 45 in.
Collection of Mr. and Mrs. Thomas B. Stiles II
(p. 80)

Sculpture ("Bird House"), c. 1925
Painted wood, 60 x 24 x 24 in.
Collection of Thomas T. Tatum
(p. 14)

Sentinels of the Coast, Monterey, 1921
Oil on canvas, 28 x 34 in.
Courtesy of The Irvine Museum
(p. 66)

Shadowed Butte, n.d.
Pencil on paper, 11 x 11 in.
Robert Giem Collection
(p. 214)

Sierra Peak, n.d.
Pencil on paper, 8 x 9 in.
Collection of John and Judith Ibbetson
(p. 71)

Sierra Peaks, c. 1919
Oil on canvas, 42 x 42 in.
Collection of D. L. Stuart Jr.
(p. 70)

Sketchbook, n.d.
Collection of Mr. and Mrs. Jon R. Stuart
(not shown)

Small Chest, n.d.
Wood, 16 x 27 x 15 in.
Courtesy of DeRu's Fine Arts
(p. 15)

Solitude's Enchantment, 1921
Oil on canvas, 43 x 43 in.
Courtesy of Edenhurst Gallery
(p. 84)

South Rim, Grand Canyon, after 1929
Oil on canvas, 25 x 30 in.
J. Dutra Collection
(p. 178 [detail], p. 198)

Stream in the Canyon, n.d.
Pencil on paper, 8 x 10½ in.
Collection of Mr. and Mrs. Jon R. Stuart
(p. 215)

Sunflowers, n.d.
Oil on canvas, 22 x 18 in.
J. Dutra Collection
(p. 230)

Sunset, Canyon de Chelly, 1916
Oil on canvas, 28 x 34 in.
Mark C. Pigott Collection
(jacket front, pp. 186–187)

Sunset in the Foothills, n.d.
Oil on canvas, 32½ x 39½ in.
Collection of D. L. Stuart Jr.
(pp. 100–101)

Swiss Village [Spiez Castle on Lake Thun], c. 1923
Oil on canvas, 28 x 34 in.
Collection of Mr. and Mrs. Jon R. Stuart
(p. 133)

Sycamore Grove, n.d.
Pencil on paper, 8 x 10 in.
Collection of Mr. and Mrs. Jon R. Stuart
(p. 31)

Sycamore in Autumn, Orange County Park, c. 1917
Oil on board, 32 x 42 in.
Private collection
Courtesy of The Irvine Museum
(p. 30, p. 242 [detail])

Three Navajo Riders, c. 1930
Photograph
Courtesy of DeRu's Fine Arts
(p. 201)

Timber Line, n.d.
Oil on canvas, 20 x 24 in.
Collection of Linda and Jim Freund
(p. 75)

Topmost Crags, 1921
Oil on canvas, 31 x 36 in.
Private collection
(pp. 82–83)

The Topmost Sierra, c. 1921
Oil on canvas, 43 x 43 in.
W. C. Foxley Collection
(p. 18 [detail], p. 74)

*Transition from Covered Wagon to Automobile in Navajo
Country*, 1920s
Photograph
Courtesy of DeRu's Fine Arts
(p. 222)

Tuna Boats, Concarneau, c. 1924
Pencil on paper, 8 x 10 in.
Courtesy of DeRu's Fine Arts
(p. 153)

Tuna Fisherman, Concarneau, c. 1924
Oil on canvas, 29 x 29 in.
Collection of Mr. and Mrs. Thomas B. Stiles II
(p. 154)

Tuna Yawls, Brittany, France, c. 1924
Photograph
Courtesy of DeRu's Fine Arts
(p. 152)

Two Indians in Southwest Landscape, after 1929
Oil on canvas, 24 x 30 in.
Collection of Mr. and Mrs. Thomas B. Stiles II
(p. 209)

Unloading Fish, Concarneau, c. 1924
Oil on canvas, 24 x 28 in.
The Edward H. and Yvonne J. Boseker Collection
(p. 170)

Untitled [Clouds and Riders], n.d.
Oil on canvas, 21½ x 21½ in.
Collection of D. L. Stuart Jr.
(p. 208)

Untitled [Eucalypti], n.d.
Oil on canvas, 28 x 32 in.
Collection of Reed and Chris Halladay
(pp. 48–49)

Untitled [Eucalyptus Landscape, California], n.d.
Oil on canvas, 32 x 40 in.
Private collection
(pp. 24–25)

Untitled [Laguna Coastal Scene], n.d.
Oil on canvas, 33 x 42 in.
Crocker Art Museum
Gift of Mrs. Charles G. Johnson, conserved with funds
provided by the Historical Collections Council of
California Art
(p. 62)

Untitled [Laguna Seascape], c. 1918
Oil on canvas, $43^{1}/_{16}$ x $43^{1}/_{8}$ in.
Collection of D. L. Stuart Jr.
(pp. 58–59)

The Valley Village, 1923
Oil on canvas on board, 29 x 29 in.
Collection of Thomas T. Tatum
(p. 139)

Venetian Boats, c. 1923
Oil on canvas, 20 x 24 in.
Collection of Mr. and Mrs. Thomas B. Stiles II
(p. 127)

A View of the Glacial Path, n.d.
Oil on canvas, 40 x 50 in.
Payton Family Collection
(pp. 42–43)

Wine Boats, Menton, c. 1923
Oil on canvas, 20 x 16 in.
The James Irvine Swinden Family Collection
(p. 120)

CONTRIBUTORS

The realization of *Edgar Payne: The Scenic Journey* and the accompanying catalogue have been made possible through the financial support of the following individuals and agencies.

Mark Pigott's presenting sponsorship of the exhibition and catalogue was invaluable and truly made this project possible.

Underwriting support has been provided by the Historical Collections Council of California Art, Barbara and Michael Brickman, Simon K. Chiu, Jeff Dutra, Robert Giem, Christine and Reed Halladay, Cathie and David Partridge, Ray Redfern of Redfern Gallery, Donna and Mark Salzberg, Mr. and Mrs. Thomas B. Stiles II, and Anonymous.

Additional support has been provided by the Jonathan Heritage Foundation, the MacTon Foundation, Kathleen and Paul Bagley, Yvonne J. Boseker, Bente and Gerald Buck, W. C. Foxley, Linda and Jim Freund, Whitney Ganz, Nadine and Robert J. Hall, Ruth and Robert Mirvis, Elma and Earl Payton, Earlene and Herb Seymour, Bernard Vandeuren, Gerard Vuilleumier, Bonhams & Butterfields, Christie's, George Stern Fine Arts, Heritage Auctions, John Moran Auctioneers, Josh Hardy Galleries, and Steven Stern, California Paintings.

We would also like to thank the individuals and institutions who generously loaned from their collections and provided images for the exhibition and catalogue, including the California State Library; the Crocker Art Museum; the Denver Art Museum; the Denver Public Library; the Frederick R. Weisman Art Museum, University of Minnesota; Hubbell Trading Post National Historic Site; the Indianapolis Museum of Art; The Irvine Museum; the Laguna Art Museum; the Los Angeles County Museum of Art; Ruth Stoever-Fleming Collection of Southern California Art; the Smithsonian American Art Museum; the Springville Museum of Art; the University of Arizona Libraries; the Utah Museum of Fine Arts, University of Utah; Kathleen and Paul Bagley; the Barnett Family; Bernadette Berger; Christopher Bliss; Yvonne J. Boseker; Bente and Gerald Buck; Simon K. Chiu; Jeff Dutra; Donna and Mort Fleischer; W. C. Foxley; Linda and Jim Freund; Robert Giem; Betty Goldfield; Nadine and Robert J. Hall; Christine and Reed Halladay; Helene Halperin; Judy and John Ibbetson; Brigitte and Martin Medak; Bette Midler and Martin Van Haselberg; Charles D. Miller; Ruth and Robert Mirvis; John Mutch; Harry Parashis; Elma and Earl Payton; Mark Pigott; Mark Sauer; Linda and Jean Stern; Mr. and Mrs. Thomas B. Stiles II; D. L. Stuart Jr.; Mr. and Mrs. Jon R. Stuart; James Irvine Swinden; Thomas T. Tatum; James Taylor and Gary Conway; Nancy and Gilbert Waldman; Julia and Roy Weinstein; Anonymous; Arizona West Galleries; Art Resource; the Bank of America Collection; BNSF Railway; Bonhams & Butterfields; DeRu's Fine Arts; Edenhurst Gallery; George Stern Fine Arts; Josh Hardy Galleries; On Foot Holidays; Redfern Gallery; Scottsdale Art Auction; Steven Stern, California Paintings; Trotter Galleries; and William A. Karges Fine Art.

ABOUT THE AUTHORS

SCOTT A. SHIELDS, PhD, Associate Director and Chief Curator of the Crocker Art Museum in Sacramento, California, is the author of numerous exhibition catalogues and books, including *Edwin Deakin: California Painter of the Picturesque* (Pomegranate) and *Artists at Continent's End: The Monterey Peninsula Art Colony, 1875–1907*.

PATRICIA TRENTON, PhD, is the editor of the landmark catalogues *Independent Spirits: Women Painters of the American West, 1890–1945* and *California Light, 1900–1930*. She has authored many books, including *Joseph Kleitsch: A Kaleidoscope of Color* and *The Rocky Mountains: A Vision for Artists in the Nineteenth Century*.

LISA N. PETERS, PhD, is Director of Research and Publications at Spanierman Gallery, New York. She has published extensively on American art from the eighteenth century to the present day, including *John Henry Twachtman: An American Impressionist* and *A Personal Gathering: Paintings and Sculpture from the Collection of William I. Koch*.

PETER H. HASSRICK is Director Emeritus of the Petrie Institute of Western American Art at the Denver Art Museum and of the Buffalo Bill Historical Center in Cody, Wyoming. He is also Founding Director Emeritus of the Charles M. Russell Center for the Study of Art of the American West, University of Oklahoma.

JEAN STERN, Executive Director of The Irvine Museum, is a recognized authority on California Impressionism and has organized many exhibitions on plein-air painting. He has published widely, most recently *Franz A. Bischoff: The Life and Art of an American Master*. He is the content editor of The Irvine Museum's series on major California artists from 1890 to 1930.

JENKINS SHANNON has served as the Executive Director of the Pasadena Museum of California Art since 2009. She has overseen numerous exhibitions examining the breadth of California art, including *Gardens & Grandeur: Porcelains and Paintings by Franz A. Bischoff* and *L.A. Raw: Abject Expressionism in Los Angeles 1945–1980, From Rico Lebrun to Paul McCarthy*.

INDEX

Page numbers in italics refer to illustrations.

Over the Hump, n.d. Oil on board, 28 x 34 in. Bank of America Collection